IN DEFENSE

of

SELFISHNESS

ALSO BY PETER SCHWARTZ

The Foreign Policy of Self-Interest: A Moral Ideal for America

Libertarianism: The Perversion of Liberty

IN DEFENSE

of

SELFISHNESS

WHY THE CODE OF SELF-SACRIFICE
IS UNJUST AND DESTRUCTIVE

PETER SCHWARTZ

palgrave
macmillan

First published in 2015 by PALGRAVE MACMILLAN® TRADE
in the United States—a division of St. Martin's Press LLC, 175 Fifth
Avenue, New York, NY 10010.

Palgrave® and Macmillan® are registered trademarks in the United States,
the United Kingdom, Europe and other countries.

ISBN: 978-1-137-28016-9

Library of Congress Cataloging-in-Publication Data

Schwartz, Peter, 1949-
    In defense of selfishness : why the code of self-sacrifice is unjust and
destructive / Peter Schwartz.
        pages cm
    ISBN 978-1-137-28016-9 (hardback)
    1. Self-interest. 2. Rand, Ayn—Philosophy. I. Title.
BJ1474.S38   2015
171'.9—dc23
                                                                    2014039801

Design by Letra Libre

First edition: June 2015

10 9 8 7 6 5 4 3 2 1

Printed in the United States of America.

To Sandra,

who makes it all possible

CONTENTS

ACKNOWLEDGEMENTS

MY GREATEST INTELLECTUAL DEBT IS TO AYN RAND. SHE formulated a comprehensive philosophy of reason and individualism, called Objectivism, which stands as the foundation upon which this book rests.

I want to thank Harry Binswanger for his perceptive suggestions concerning my discussion of altruism's philosophic history.

Yaron Brook, president of the Ayn Rand Institute, deserves a great deal of credit for seeing the value of this book early on, and for his continuing assistance along its path to publication. While the whole Institute has been supportive, I'd like to single out the following people there: Jason Eriksen, Michael Spicci, David Antonacci and Simon Federman for helping the book gain Internet exposure; Lin Zinser for her general publicity work; and Mark Chapman for overseeing much of this effort.

I am grateful to Mary Ann Sures for the quiet, benevolent encouragement she would convey to me from time to time during the writing process.

A great deal of research was required, much of which was ably and conscientiously provided by Barbara Nelson. Other researchers who assisted at various times were Carl Svanberg, Naama Tal, Miki Jeshurun, Jennifer Peterson and Jenniffer Woodson.

At Palgrave Macmillan, two individuals in particular have earned my gratitude: Karen Wolny, editorial director, who helped make this a better product; and Alan Bradshaw, production manager, who scrupulously shepherded this work in its trek from manuscript to book.

I should also thank my literary agent, Scott Mendel. After making many unsuccessful attempts to secure an agent, I was impressed by Scott's optimistic view of the book's commercial potential. When I sent him my proposal, he read it immediately and took me on as a client the very next day. He assured me he would have little difficulty finding a good publisher—and less than a week later, Palgrave Macmillan bought the book.

In this list of acknowledgements, I leave for last the person who represents my most selfish value: my wife, Sandra. The dedication page expresses the essence of my relationship with her. Here, I simply thank her for doing the demanding work of preparing the index.

IN DEFENSE

of

SELFISHNESS

INTRODUCTION

EVERY CIVILIZED CULTURE IS SHAPED BY SOME VIEW OF right and wrong. While there will always be people who simply are amoral, such as criminals, they are the exception and they do not influence a culture's direction. If a society predominantly rejects morality, it quickly disintegrates into savage, warring gangs. Thus, in every culture, although disagreements can abound concerning the means of implementation, there must be widespread acceptance of some fundamental ethical principle. In ours, it is the principle of altruism.

Whenever we are exhorted to do what is trumpeted as morally right—"give to the homeless," "preserve the safety net," "shrink the inequality of incomes"—it is the code of self-sacrifice that is being invoked. Some people may comply wholeheartedly, many may comply grudgingly, others may not comply at all—but virtually everyone believes the altruist code to be correct. Non-compliers, feeling guilty, may come up with various rationalizations for their failure to obey such exhortations, but few will offer any moral objections. Few will challenge the moral validity of the idea that the needs of others should take precedence over one's own interests.

In this book you will find the reasons to challenge it.

My purpose is to alter your view of altruism and of selfishness—not just your evaluation of them, but your understanding of what these two concepts actually mean. Here, for example, are some common beliefs about altruism:

- Adopting altruism is the way to achieve social harmony.
- Altruism underlies such basic virtues as honesty and integrity.
- The public interest clashes with private interests.
- Love and friendship are rooted in altruism.
- There is no moral alternative to the code of self-sacrifice.

And here are some common beliefs about selfishness:

- Selfishness is typified by the predatory behavior of thugs and con men.
- Only materialistic values are compatible with selfishness.
- The greed of businessmen leads to shoddy and unsafe products.
- The pursuit of self-interest requires the renunciation of moral principles.

All these beliefs are mistaken—and the task of this book is to undo such misconceptions. This book demonstrates, in both theory and practice, the iniquity of altruism. It reveals the lack of any validation for altruism's demands, whether voiced by liberals who urge us to sacrifice in order to provide for the uninsured or by conservatives who urge us to sacrifice in order to preserve the traditions of our community. Using vivid, real-life examples, this book explains why the continual social conflicts we experience are primarily a result, not of the absence of altruism in our lives, but of its overwhelming presence. And it offers a genuine, non-predatory alternative—an alternative that creates a harmony of interests among people—based on Ayn Rand's ethics of rational self-interest.

Our society takes as a given the idea that pursuing your own welfare is morally tainted but sacrificing yourself for the benefit of others is virtuous. *In Defense of Selfishness: Why the Code of Self-Sacrifice Is Unjust and Destructive* asks you to question that assumption.

ONE

THE SHACKLES

YES—I'M DEFENDING *SELFISHNESS*.

Let's first examine what I'm defending it against.

People disagree on a vast range of important issues. They argue over whether God exists, whether man has free will, whether capitalism is superior to socialism, whether rights pertain to fetuses. But one crucial question generates almost no debate: the question of whether self-sacrifice is morally good. Sacrificing yourself for the needs of others is universally seen as the essence of morality. The tenets of altruism are widely regarded not simply as true, but as practically self-evident. Acting for the benefit of others is deemed virtuous, while acting for your own benefit is not. People may, of course, choose not to behave ethically, but they take as incontrovertible the premise that if one *does* wish to be ethical one must be altruistic. Even questioning this premise is, to most people, equivalent to entertaining the notion that the earth is flat.

Why?

Altruism is commonly viewed as a proscription against preying on other people. It is taken as a demand that we refrain from acting like Attila the Hun—that we respect each other's rights and avoid victimizing anyone in pursuit of our goals. Altruism, it is held, keeps us from one another's throats, and leads to a benevolent, harmonious society.

But does it—or does it lead to the opposite?

Consider the doctrine's actual meaning. It tells you to *subordinate* yourself to other people. It tells you that in any choice you make, your own interests should be less important to you than those of someone else. It tells you that if others have less than you, you are duty-bound to provide for them. Thus, no matter how diligently you may have worked to earn your money, every time you spend it on yourself rather than on the needy—and there is always somebody, somewhere whose unfulfilled needs you can meet—you are acting immorally. To comply with the demands of altruism, you must sacrifice your wealth, your goals, your interests. If you have something people lack, you must grant them moral priority. You must be willing, that is, to *serve* others.

ALTRUISM AS SERVITUDE

Let's look at some real-life examples.

Suppose you are a serious, industrious high school student. You study hard to achieve good grades, you prepare to get into a top college, you work at part-time jobs to save money. But since many high schools now require students to spend significant time performing so-called community service in order to graduate, you may be informed that your single-minded concern with your own life is morally unacceptable. Only if you sacrifice that concern—only if you take time away from your studies and your future in favor of, say, cleaning bedpans in a hospital ward—will you be declared worthy of a diploma.

Or suppose you are a dentist at the height of the AIDS epidemic. Your patient informs you that she has the HIV virus. To protect yourself against possible infection, you offer to treat her in a hospital, rather than in your office. But she refuses. Instead, she sues you, arguing that the law requires "equal treatment" for those with disabilities, such as the HIV virus—and that if non-HIV patients are treated in your office, the same must be done for HIV patients. The courts rule in favor of the plaintiff. You are told that the needs of those deemed disabled take precedence over concerns about your own safety.[1]

Or suppose you are a budding athlete. If your team wins some tournament, trophies will likely be given, not just to you and your teammates, but to all the players of all the teams equally, in the form of what are disingenuously called participation awards. The achievers of victory are deliberately not rewarded, in order to accommodate the needs of the non-achievers. Taking the idea of self-sacrifice further, one youth hockey league declares that if you are an excellent player you will be suspended if your team is not losing enough games. A team that is doing too well is barred by rule from competition unless it gets rid of its best player. According to a league official: "The spirit of the rule is every team in every organization wins and loses about the same number of games."[2] That rule reflects the canon of altruism. It reflects, not the understandable desire for competitive matches, but the egalitarian hostility toward unequal outcomes. It orders you to give up what you personally value—the attainment of victory—and defer to the needs of those unable to win on their own merit. Because you have the ability to succeed, you must sacrifice for those who do not.

In your dealings with people, it is not generosity that altruism wants to elicit from you. Generosity is a *gift*. What altruism demands is the payment of a *debt*—an unchosen moral debt you owe to others.

If your neighbor's house is ravaged by fire, it is perfectly appropriate for you, as a *non-altruist*, to choose to help the victim by bringing him, say, a hot meal or a spare cot. Because you value *your* life, because you value the fact that *you* are a human being, you attach a certain value even to strangers, since they have the same fundamental nature as you and potentially share your basic values. In various situations, therefore, you may be willing to help people in a spirit of true, non-sacrificial goodwill. But your assistance is not prompted by any innate obligation you have toward others. Your premise is that it is your money and your time—which you generously decide you can spare, and for which the recipient should be grateful. You don't make yourself starve so that your neighbor can eat. You don't make your children go homeless so that his children can be sheltered. Nor do you provide help to someone *undeserving* of it, such as a habitual drunkard who, in an alcoholic stupor, has burned down his own house (and may burn down yours next).

Altruism, however, takes as its premise that your money and your time are not yours, but belong to anyone with an unmet need. Altruism wants you to spend money or time you *cannot* spare. "True charity"—according to an apocryphal statement, sometimes attributed to Gandhi—"is not just giving a man a dime when he is hungry. It is giving a man a dime when you are as hungry as he is and need the dime just as badly."[3] Why is another's hunger more important than yours in determining how to spend your dime? Because—the altruist code contends—you have an intrinsic *duty* to serve others. That is, you must concede to them a right to your possessions and you must disregard your own well-being in favor of theirs.

Whatever adjectives characterize human relations under such a doctrine, "benevolent" and "harmonious" are surely not among them.

Under the mandate of self-sacrifice, need constitutes an unassailable claim, and you must surrender your values whenever that claim is presented against you. Consider some other real-life instances of altruism:

- A business student, allegedly suffering from "dyscalculia"—
  an inability to solve mathematical problems—demands an
  exemption from a required math-related course. The college
  is ordered by the federal Department of Education to provide
  for the student's needs and to waive the requirement.[4]

- A law school graduate, asserting that a deficiency in reading skills made her fail the New York Bar exam three times, insists that she be allowed unlimited time to take the test and that she be given a stenographer to record her answers. A court rules that her needs entitle her to those accommodations, as well as to compensatory damages.[5]
- The president of the New York City Chapter of the National Federation of the Blind opposes the airlines' policy of keeping blind people from sitting in emergency-evacuation rows. He claims that such a policy "relegates[s] the blind to an inferior status in society."[6] And a bill in the U.S. Senate seeks to enact his view into law.[7] In other words, the blind have needs, which must supersede all other considerations, including the safety of a plane's passengers.

In all these cases, the assumption is that the demands of the needy must be met. Regardless of the suffering imposed upon you, you may not refuse those demands. Need—it is believed—is a moral absolute.

THE PERVERSE MEANING OF "NEED"

But, you might ask, if need is the overriding factor, what about *your* needs? Why is it right for you to fulfill the needs of someone else, but wrong to fulfill your own?

That is, the dental patient may feel a need to be dealt with as if she did not have the HIV virus—but what about the dentist's need to guard against a potentially dangerous disease? Why is that ignored by altruism? Some of the hockey league's athletes may feel a need to pretend that their victories are meaningful once the better players have been removed—but what about the need of the conscientious player, of whatever ability, to enjoy authentic competition in pursuit of authentic victories? A deficient student may feel a need to be granted special accommodations by his school—but what about the need of a capable student to obtain a degree unadulterated by the lowered standards? What about the need of the school to have its degree be an objective indicator of performance, rather than a token document? What about the need of prospective employers and clients to know the actual level of ability of a school's graduates? Why, in other words, are only some needs and not others granted the moral right-of-way?

The answer is that under altruism only one thing qualifies as a need: *that which requires someone else's sacrifice to fulfill.*

If your needs can be satisfied by your own effort, altruism dismisses them. If you take responsibility for your life and support it by your own work, if you deal with others through trade and offer them equal value in exchange for what they give you, altruism takes no cognizance of your needs. If, however, you fail to undertake that responsibility—if you wish to deal with others without offering them value for value, if you want a meal not by paying for it but by having someone give you his, if you seek to be sustained not by what you have produced but by what others have sacrificed for you—only then does altruism declare that you have needs, and that they are sacrosanct.

Think about the previous examples. The dentist is not asking for any sacrifice from the patient. Once the two cannot agree on a mutually beneficial exchange, he wants only to be left alone. He seeks nothing from her *that he does not already have;* his need to remain safe from infection does not require her to give him anything. She, however, does want a sacrifice. She demands the benefit of the knowledge he has acquired and the skills he has mastered, on terms he finds unacceptable. She wants him to give up what is his because she is in need. This is why her wishes carry moral weight, according to altruism, while his are irrelevant.

Similarly, the conscientious hockey player's need for an opportunity to compete, by doing his best and reaping the rewards of his work, does not require another's act of sacrifice. In normal, non-altruistic competition, the opponent is not sacrificing when he is fairly defeated—any more than you are sacrificing when you refrain from stealing your neighbor's car, since the car is not yours to give up. The loser is not entitled to victory, and so is not sacrificing it. The winning hockey team *earns* its triumph. This is why altruism has no concern for the superior player. But with respect to some inferior player's need to be handed an unearned victory—a victory based not on justice but on pity, a victory he obtains not by applying his talent and effort, but by having his opponents prohibited from applying theirs—altruism is eager to satisfy it, for it is a need that can be fulfilled only through an act of sacrifice. By whom? By those who are entitled to victory, and are being asked to give it up. Asked, by whom? By those who do not deserve it, but who *need* it.

This is the meaning of need, as enshrined by altruism.

Consequently, students who seek degrees they do not deserve, or blind passengers who seek exit-row seats they are not qualified to occupy, are regarded by the altruist as manifesting needs. Whereas competent students who want degrees that reflect their actual accomplishments, or airline passengers who have contracted for a safe flight and want the emergency-exit seats assigned to people able to facilitate urgent evacuations, are not asking for sacrifices and so are deemed to be exhibiting, not needs, but merely selfish desires.

Under altruism, therefore, society is divided into two classes: those who have needs, and those who are able—and thus required—to fulfill them.

It is not even that altruism pretends to somehow measure—impossible as that would be—one person's need against another's, with the larger need prevailing. It is not that altruism professes to calculate, say, that the patient's need to have a tooth fixed at one location rather than another is greater than the dentist's need to be shielded against a dangerous disease. Rather, the altruist maintains that the only *real* need is the patient's, since its fulfillment requires a sacrifice by the dentist. And since need is the paramount factor, whoever possesses something of value ought to surrender it to whoever lacks it.

Again, your perplexed reaction to this must be to ask: Why? Why is it a virtue to surrender what you've earned so that others might enjoy it, but a vice to keep it for your own pleasure? Why should the needs of others be the standard in ethics? Why should your ability to achieve something become a leash around your neck? Why should morality demand that you suffer for the sake of any non-you?

The issue is not whether to help someone in distress—that's window dressing. The sole issue is whether you have a moral *duty* to others. Is your life yours, or does anyone with a need have a claim to it? Do you have a right to live for your own sake, or is serving your fellow-man the moral purpose and justification of your existence?

When altruism instructs you to sacrifice for someone in need, it does not matter that you did not cause the other person's plight. It does not even matter if that person is himself the willful generator, and perpetuator, of his troubles. The sheer fact of need, regardless of its cause, is all that counts. If a food-stamp recipient spends his days studying the racing forms rather than the help-wanted ads, if a sixteen-year-old high school dropout demands rent for a new apartment because she is pregnant with her third child, if a homeless man regularly buys crack with the handouts he receives—you are still duty-bound to provide for them. The fact that you think they do not deserve your help only makes your assistance that much more of a sacrifice. And the greater the sacrifice being demanded of you, the greater must be the recipient's need and therefore the greater the imperative that you fulfill it.

The primary object of altruism's concern is not the innocent victim of some misfortune. To the contrary, it is the genuinely guilty—the person who deserves no sympathy whatever, but who desperately *needs* it—who becomes the poster child for the cause of altruism.

When the twenty-year-old daughter of Bob and Golden Bristol was savagely raped and strangled to death in California, the couple publicly embraced the convicted murderer by announcing: "We love this special person from the bottom of our hearts." When the judge who sentenced the perpetrator to life imprisonment described him as "the most vicious killer I have encountered in my career," the forgiving couple, faithfully practicing the code of altruism, said: "We view this person as one of value and worth . . . not for what he did, but for what he can become."[8] By the standard of justice and loyalty to the memory of their daughter, they should have condemned the creature who took a precious value away from them. Altruism, however, demanded something else. It demanded that they be concerned, not with their own values, but with the needs of the killer.

The less deserving the recipient, the more self-sacrificial your aid—and the more obligated you are to offer it. This altruistic principle is behind the Biblical injunctions to "turn the other cheek" and to "love thy enemy." To love a friend is in your interest. But to love an enemy—to love those who wish you harm—to *welcome* their harming you—that is a true act of altruism.

It is an act reflecting the primacy—and the tyranny—of need.

THE OMNIPRESENCE OF ALTRUISM

But do these illustrations represent only the exceptions? Don't most people reject altruism in their daily lives and instead pursue their own practical interests? Doesn't the abundance of wealth in this country attest to the fact that far more people want to be like Bill Gates than like Mother Teresa? Why then make such an issue about the oppressiveness of altruism?

Because altruism is accepted even by those who routinely fail to practice it.

To breach some creed is not necessarily to repudiate it. While most Americans probably do wish to grow rich, they nonetheless accept the altruist's evaluation of that desire as crude and ignoble. People contravene the code of altruism continually—as they must, if they wish to live—but they refuse to challenge its validity. They remain unwilling to replace it with a different code. Every step they take toward emulating Bill Gates is weighted down by the leg-irons of altruism.

Look at Gates himself, a man who has worked to become a multi-billionaire. What is he most proud of morally? Not that he has created an inventive array of products that have enhanced the lives of virtually everyone in the industrialized world, but that he has established a charitable foundation to give away his money. It is philanthropy that he exhorts people to take up as a crusade. Morally, the benefits achieved by Microsoft are regarded as the tainted detritus of self-interest.

Or look at the co-chairman of Gates' charitable foundation, his father, William Gates, Sr. The elder Gates belongs to an organization called Responsible Wealth, which consists of some of the richest people in the country, such as Warren Buffett, Ted Turner and George Soros. Prompted by proposals to repeal the estate tax, these billionaires launched a campaign—*against* repeal. They want the government to compel you, and them, to continue sacrificing. They argue that you are not entitled to bequeath your wealth to your chosen heirs; instead, it ought to be transferred by government to its rightful owners: the needy.[9]

Regardless of how actively people work to advance their self-interest, most still accept—even if unenthusiastically—the belief that those who have more ought to serve those who have less. They still regard self-sacrifice as a virtue. They may frequently break the commandments of altruism, but in doing so they exhibit self-recrimination, not self-assertiveness. Like a religious person who has sinned, they reproach themselves for their shortcomings. They may wish to become as rich as Gates, but it is Mother Teresa who still stands as their ethical ideal. And, since no straitjacket is as restricting as the self-imposed bindings of guilt, their failure to live up to that ideal only reinforces altruism's grip over them.

They can resist that grip half-heartedly, they can resist it furtively—but they are unable to resist it openly and self-confidently. They may be willing to transgress behind closed doors, but not out in the public square. If they have to defend themselves against accusations of selfishness, they are helpless. Thus, when the political system proclaims that everyone should sacrifice, they cannot overtly oppose such demands.

And those demands are everywhere.

Government officials constantly take money from one person in order to provide for the needs of others. They take it on behalf of the

Nebraska farmers who need subsidies to grow corn, the New York City commuters who need subsidies to keep their subways running, the Illinois refineries that need subsidies to produce ethanol, the San Francisco artists who need subsidies to stage presentations of their inscrutable work. Your money is taken in order to provide various people with drug-rehabilitation counseling, social recreation centers, cell phones, mortgages, tennis courts and rural airline service. It is taken to provide foreign aid to impoverished nations, whose authoritarian rulers—having rejected the political freedom that makes your prosperity possible—are permitted to lay claim to your wealth by pointing to two vital facts about it: that you have it and that they need it.

Our public officials regularly promulgate such policies, and our citizens regularly tolerate them. Why? Because of the hold of altruism. Do you yourself not have uses for all the money that is being seized from you? Your interests are immaterial, the altruist says: money that is earned by one individual ought to be spent on the needs of another.

People may raise practical objections to such programs, but does anyone question their moral *rightness?* People may criticize the means, but does anyone challenge the *ends?* Does anyone openly renounce the creed of self-sacrifice? No such voices are heard— because altruism pervades our culture.

The distinguishing characteristic of a servant is that he works not for his own benefit, but for someone else's. He is ruled by the needs of his master. Is that essentially different from the relationship prescribed by altruism? Doesn't altruism give one person the moral right to direct the efforts of another? The person in need commands; the person able to satisfy that need obeys.

Altruism is ultimately a call for servitude. It is the admonition that you subjugate yourself to others. It is the insistence that you be shackled to their needs. It is the demand, not that you respect other people's property—but that you *become* their property.

This is what it means to espouse self-sacrifice as virtue.

There is no rational explanation for such a doctrine. Nothing can validate it. There is no logical justification for man to regard himself as a sacrificial animal.

Why, then, is the altruist ethics so widely accepted? Because the alleged alternative to altruism—the alternative of selfishness, which is universally condemned as evil—has been made into a straw man.

TWO

THE STRAW MAN

WHAT CONVEYS TO YOU THE QUINTESSENCE OF SELFISH-
ness? If you are typical, you picture some brainless brute, raping and
pillaging at will. Or perhaps you picture a scheming con man, callously cheating widows and orphans out of their last pennies. You
regard selfishness, in other words, as personified by some amoral mis-
creant, who readily lies, steals and kills in order to gratify his desires.

Yet the term "selfishness" means only a concern with one's own
interests. To be selfish is simply to care about one's own life. If so,
what about all the people who support their lives and pursue their
well-being by their own efforts *without* victimizing others? What
about all the individuals who seek their self-interest, not by parasitically feeding off others, but by *earning* what they get? The mailroom
clerk who works diligently for his paycheck; the college student who
spends his time studying rather than partying; the athlete training
tirelessly to make himself a champion; the inventor who devotes

himself to the goal of becoming rich by devising a better mousetrap; the artist dedicated to creating a work that fully meets his independent standards—these are all examples of selfishness. These are all people who are acting to improve *their* lives by pursuing *their* goals. But they are not benefiting at the expense of others. Their method of living is to produce (and trade for) the things they value, not to seize them from others. *This* type of behavior is the appropriate referent for the concept of selfishness.

But the advocates of altruism do not want us to think that selfishness applies to anyone who attains his ends without injuring others. Although there is an obvious difference between a producer and a predator—between a Warren Buffett and a Bernard Madoff, between someone who *makes* money and someone who steals it—this distinction is regularly blurred. Instead, the two types are lumped together into one wooly package-deal. Since the predator is committing a moral crime, we are told, so is everyone who pursues self-interested ends.

SELFISHNESS MISDEFINED

Altruism's purveyors want, in effect, to entrench Attila the Hun as the paradigm of selfishness. They try to equate selfishness with the destruction of others. Note how some dictionaries have slipped this notion into the very definition of "selfish." *Webster's New Collegiate Dictionary,* for example, defines it as "regarding one's own comfort, advantage, etc., *in disregard, or at the expense, of that of others*" (emphasis added). Defining selfishness in this manner makes it seem that the harming of others is an integral part of the concept. It suggests that one man's gain is possible only through another's loss. It implies that the only choice you have is to sacrifice yourself to others, by being altruistic, or to sacrifice others to yourself, by being selfish. It presents, as exemplars of this false alternative, a Mother Teresa, humbly sacrificing herself in service to others, and an Attila, viciously sacrificing others in service to himself. But what about the category of self-responsible, self-supporting individuals, who thrive without asking for or offering sacrifices? No such classification exists, according to the altruists.

The issue of selfishness has, of course, been a central topic in intellectual history. Various theories of egoism—the view that selfishness is good—have been propounded over the years. But ever since the end of the Classical era in Greece, the dominant viewpoint, even among the putative *defenders* of egoism, has been that selfishness is typified by an impulsive, unconstrained fiend who tramples over others to reach his ends. For example, the nineteenth-century philosopher Friedrich Nietzsche, who is most identified with this view, held that self-interest calls for some people to rule others. Selfishness, he said, consists of a "will to power," which is exercised by those—the "*uber*men"—who are entitled to enslave others as a means to their "superior" ends. "What is good?" Nietzsche asked rhetorically. "All that heightens the feeling of power, the will to power, power itself in man." His heroes are authoritarian rulers like Caesar and Napoleon, who are "beyond good and evil."[1] They are guided by their desires, unimpeded by considerations of right and wrong.

With defenders like Nietzsche, it is no surprise that egoism has been roundly rejected by thinkers. Prevailing opinion has come to concur with Thomas Hobbes, the seventeenth-century philosopher who contended that selfishness leads to unrestrained savagery and anarchy. He believed that you will always crave what someone else has, and that self-interest obliges you to grab it. The result: a war of all against all. According to Hobbes, "If any two men desire the same thing, which nevertheless they cannot both enjoy, they . . . endeavor to destroy or subdue one another." If allowed to be guided by self-interest, he said, "every man is enemy to every man," with life ending up being "solitary, poor, nasty, brutish and short."[2] The only way to preserve civilized society, he insisted, is to establish an absolute state, which would then rein in the individual's animalistic desires.

With the influence of Christianity, this portrait of man has held sway throughout post-Greek history. Accepting the idea of Original Sin and the innate depravity of man, people interpreted selfishness as the unleashing of that depravity—for which the only corrective was the shackles of altruism. The Attila-type, the rabid emotionalist who acts on whatever desires he happens to experience, thus became the accepted embodiment of egoism.

In the mid-twentieth century, however, a radically different perspective was introduced. Ayn Rand originated a philosophy, Objectivism, with a new conception of selfishness.

In broad terms her view is similar to that of Aristotle, who, in the fourth century B.C., espoused a form of rational egoism. He maintained that the good is the achievement of one's own happiness, as determined by reason. However, he could not fully prove his position. He could not objectively justify his standard of value or validate the virtues he endorsed.

Rand too presents an ethics of egoism based on the idea of man as a rational being. But her approach is to start by identifying the facts of reality that generate the need for a code of values in the first place. She shows how an "ought" is logically derived from an "is"—how the very concept of "value" is given rise to by, and has no meaning apart from, the concept of "life." It is only to a living organism, she argues—only to an entity facing a conditional existence, which has to be sustained through self-generated action—that something can be good or bad. And the standard of value, therefore, is the life of the organism: that which sustains the organism's life is good, that which harms it is bad.[3]

I won't go into the full explication of this system of ethics. Our main concern here is Rand's novel view of the nature of self-interest.

RATIONAL SELFISHNESS

What constitutes a person's self-interest? It cannot be the fulfillment of whatever he happens to desire. After all, there are people who desire to be drug addicts, alcoholics, masochists, serial killers. People behave in countless ways that are patently against their interests. Just as ingesting anything we wish will not meet our nutritional needs, doing whatever strikes our fancy will not meet our interests in general. Life has *objective* requirements. Some actions promote our interests, while others harm them—regardless of our wishes.

Is there, then, some fundamental course of action on which human life depends? Yes, says Rand: one that is driven by a commitment to rationality. While animals are automatically programmed for survival, man is not. The knowledge of how to plant a crop or build a house or cure an infection does not come from some inborn instinct. How does man discover what is good for him and what is bad? By his faculty of reason. He must *think* in order to live. Every choice man faces rests on the choice of whether to focus his mind and grasp the facts of reality or to keep his mind unfocused and defy reality. He needs to eat—should he work for his sustenance or wait for manna to descend from heaven? He is sick—should he find a doctor or rely on a faith-healer? He is tempted to risk his life savings on a roll of the dice—should he follow his intellect or trust in his horoscope's assurance that it is his lucky day? He has a lifetime ahead of him—should he plan what to make of his future or drift unthinkingly from moment to random moment? "For man," Rand maintains, "the basic means of survival is *reason*."[4]

A person may *wish* to take a certain action; he may *hope* the action benefits him; he may *fear* to consider an alternative. But feelings cannot substitute for the process of *thought* that will tell him whether the action is in fact helpful or harmful to him. Refusing to think—elevating emotions above the verdicts of one's mind, willfully disdaining the truth, evading the fact that driving while drunk is dangerous or the fact that the object one is snatching belongs by right to someone else—is the path to self-destruction. Our self-interest is achieved, not when we blindly act on our desires, but when we act on the firm knowledge that our desires are valid. Our self-interest is achieved when reason informs us that our ideas and our values are consonant with the demands of reality and with our nature as human beings.

A state of mindlessness is a state of disregard for one's own well-being. The whim-driven Attilas of the world are acting in contradiction to their long-term interests. To be selfish is to be rational. And to be rational is to understand the principle that each individual ought to live through the reasoning, and by the products, of his own mind. Which means that, when interacting with people, one disavows reason's antithesis: force. To be rational is to deal with others by persuasion, not coercion—by trade, not theft.

A predator, such as Attila, is contemptible not because he is acting on behalf of his own interests, but because of what he wrongly believes those interests to be. His evil lies not in the desire to advance his own welfare, but in the irrational notion that the way to advance it is through plunder. The truly selfish individual does not live by expropriating the products of others; nor, concomitantly, does he grant anyone the moral right to expropriate his.

An excellent concretization of the meaning of selfishness is provided by the character of Howard Roark, the hero of Ayn Rand's novel *The Fountainhead*. Roark is an innovative architect, who challenges the traditions of his field and follows nothing but his own independent judgment. He has scrupulously thought out his standards, in architecture and in life, and refuses to compromise them. His intransigence provokes wide-ranging antagonism. He is hindered, shunned, ridiculed and denounced. He is continually exhorted to stop being so unyielding, to defer to the needs and the opinions of others, to temper his rectitude, to give in. But he remains true—selfishly true—to his own convictions.

In one telling scene, set early in his career, Roark finds himself no longer able to obtain clients; his architectural style is regarded as too unconventional. He is behind on the rent for his office and for his apartment. He has pawned his watch. His telephone is about to be disconnected. He has fourteen dollars to his name. But he has one last chance, the possibility of a major commission from a bank. He has submitted drawings for a fifty-story structure to be built in the center of Manhattan, and has been waiting, day after day, for a decision. Finally, he is called to a meeting by the bank's officers, who tell him that his proposal has been accepted—"on one minor condition." To accommodate their fear that the public will be put off by his non-traditional design, he must append to his modern building an incongruous, Classic Greek façade.

Roark resolutely tries to make them understand why his design should be kept intact:

> He spoke for a long time. He explained why this structure could not have a Classic motive on its façade. He explained why an honest building, like an honest man, had to be of one piece and one faith; what constituted the life source, the idea in any existing

thing or creature, and why—if one smallest part committed treason to that idea—the thing or the creature was dead; and why the good, the high and the noble on earth was only that which kept its integrity.

But the chairman rebuffs his attempt:

"I'm sorry, Mr. Roark, but the board will not re-open the question for further debate. It was final. I can only ask you to state whether you agree to accept the commission on our terms or not. . . . You understand the situation, Mr. Roark?"

"Yes," said Roark. His eyes were lowered. He was looking down at the drawings.

"Well?"

Roark did not answer.

"Yes or no, Mr. Roark?"

Roark's head leaned back. He closed his eyes.

"No," said Roark.

Dumbfounded by the decision, one of the company's officers implores Roark to reconsider:

"It's sheer insanity!" [the officer] moaned. "I want you. We want your building. You need the commission. Do you have to be quite so fanatical and selfless about it?"

"What?" Roark asked incredulously.

"Fanatical and selfless."

Roark smiled. He looked down at his drawings. His elbow moved a little, pressing them to his body. He said:

"That was the most selfish thing you've ever seen a man do."[5]

This is what selfishness means. Roark is unwilling to compromise his architectural vision. It is *his* vision, and he will not give it up just because people disagree with him. The integrity of his work means everything to him, and he will not forfeit it simply to obtain a commission—a commission whose entire purpose is to enable him to do the kind of work he fundamentally values. To be selfish is to regard your life as something precious, as something to be passionately embraced, not self-effacingly surrendered. To be selfish is to strive to achieve the best that is possible to you. To be selfish is to remain loyal to your ideals.

Yet the altruists disparage selfishness as vile.

When Roark ultimately triumphs, when he surmounts the social opposition and establishes himself as a successful architect, it is by not leeching off others. He prevails not by copying the blueprints of his rivals, but by originating his own. He designs his kind of buildings and eventually finds clients who recognize the value of his work. Roark determinedly seeks his own happiness, but knows that it can be generated only by his own achievements.

Yet the altruists disparage selfishness as exploitative.

It is not that they try to prove that people like Howard Roark are evil. Doing so would acknowledge that there is indeed a conception of selfishness exemplified by Roark—an acknowledgement they are unwilling to make. Rather, they assert their claims not through argument but through obfuscation. They fabricate a straw man to represent selfishness. They concoct a linguistic jumble, in which selfishness is fuzzily *defined* as the depredations of a predator, so that any action intended to benefit oneself rather than others is considered wicked.

Our concepts shape our cognition, and there is simply no concept, in common usage, that refers to actual, i.e., non-predatory, selfishness. The word that should identify the behavior of an honest producer is used instead to identify only the behavior of an unprincipled parasite.

Imagine that there was confusion about the concept "food." Imagine that it was being defined as "anything one swallows," so that there was no distinction between a cup of soup and a cup of arsenic. For those who accepted this package-deal, the genuine meaning of food, as containing nutrients, would be lost. Instead, they would find themselves confronting a dubious choice: eat—and die of poison; or refrain from eating—and die of starvation. The same kind of false alternative is being presented here: be selfish—and make others into your servants; or be unselfish—and make yourself into theirs.

The authentic concept of selfishness, of simply pursuing one's interests, has been surreptitiously expunged from our vocabulary. The promoters of altruism are guilty not of an error, but of a fraud, a gigantic distortion in which the very language by which any discussion of the merits of altruism versus egoism could be conducted has been lost. There is no way to debate whether it is proper to live selfishly, as a Howard Roark does, if the concept that ought to refer to the rational, productive, self-reliant individual has been redefined out of existence.

THE SELFISHNESS OF LOVE

The altruists' deception is abetted by the notion that selfishness requires utter indifference to other people. This notion assumes that a selfish individual has only materialistic concerns. It assumes that true friendship or romance cannot be in anybody's self-interest, and that one would have to become a misanthropic recluse to embrace selfishness. In fact, though, one's self-interest is fueled by both material and spiritual values. A moment's thought would reveal that there is a vast benefit *to you* in having a friend or a lover. You choose relationships with people who are important—*to you*. You choose to give your affection to those who mean something—*to you*.

Now, if you heeded the altruists and gave your love indiscriminately—if such was even possible—you would indeed be acting selflessly. To love a stranger—or an enemy—*is* an act of self-abnegation. But genuine love is not selfless; it is not dispensed as alms. Consider the absurdity of declaring that you love someone, not because of anything worthwhile in him or her, but purely as an act of charity. It's an absurdity because love is given, not in pity, but in response to a person's value to you. And, as a result, it offers you an exquisite joy. To love your spouse, to love the person with whom you wish to spend your life, to love the one who embodies the things you treasure most—is an intensely personal, *selfish* choice. It is only the disgraceful misrepresentations by altruists that could make one regard love, or any positive human relationship, as self-sacrificial.

The distortions about selfishness are further facilitated by the warped meaning attached to the concept "sacrifice." What does this term actually denote? Clearly, it cannot refer simply to giving up something. After all, every gainful trade involves giving up something, such as when you give up money to buy a meal. But in a trade, you are giving up what you value less in exchange for what you value more. The term "sacrifice," by contrast, denotes the opposite: relinquishing something of value to you for the sake of something that is not. To sacrifice is to suffer a loss—which is, of course, precisely why altruism considers it a virtue. The high school student who is told to give up his personal pursuits and mop floors at a soup kitchen instead, is being told to sacrifice. The child who is urged by his mother to share his favorite toy with the nasty, whining brat who keeps trying to break it, is being urged to sacrifice. The worker who gives a drunken vagrant part of his paycheck, because he feels guilty for having something that the vagrant lacks, is making a sacrifice. These are all instances in which a person harms himself so that someone else might benefit.

Today, however, the term "sacrificing" has been twisted to mean forgoing a short-term pleasure for a long-term gain. The enormous effort someone devotes to becoming a brain surgeon or a concert violinist is labeled a sacrifice, when in fact it reflects the opposite:

a far-sighted plan designed to yield maximum rewards—*selfish* rewards, both material and spiritual—in the future. A chess player who gives up a rook in order to ultimately capture his opponent's queen is not sacrificing—he is *profiting* by the move; only if he deliberately loses the game out of pity for a needy opponent is he sacrificing. The soldier of a free country who chooses to fight when his nation is under military attack is not sacrificing—he is defending *his* freedom and that of *his* loved ones against those who want to destroy it; only if he risks his life for a so-called humanitarian purpose, such as keeping primitive tribes from massacring one another in some remote conflict that has no bearing on his own life, is he sacrificing.

Obliterating this distinction means that every investment you make—every decision to refrain from consuming a dollar now so that you can have two dollars in the future—is a sacrifice, no different from giving away your dollars forever by becoming your brother's keeper and bankroller.

If giving up a momentary pleasure for a long-term benefit is considered a sacrifice, then it follows that indulging in such pleasure, at the price of the long-term benefit, will be labeled an act of selfishness.

For example, a front-page newspaper story about a football team features the headline: "Selfishness Gets the Blame." The article states that when the players were asked why the team was doing so badly, "selfishness was cited repeatedly as the reason." Various team members, it was said, are "not at home getting rest, studying film or their playbooks when they're out into the wee hours of the morning and getting into trouble." Such players "are viewed as selfish by their teammates."[6] So giving in to a desire to spend the evening getting drunk, thereby impairing one's ability to perform during the next day's game, is supposedly selfish, while staying sober, in order to be able to take the actions that lead to personal success in one's profession, is somehow selfless.

Short-sighted, self-destructive businesses are similarly accused of being selfish. A business that foolishly tries to save a few dollars by cutting back on the quality or safety of its product, causing it to lose customers and eventually go bankrupt, is characteristically regarded as being too greedy. The mindless pursuit of fleeting gains in disregard of the consequences, whether done by a brutal Attila or by his more mannered cousin, the conniving fly-by-nighter, is now interpreted as the essence of selfishness. Despite the fact that engaging in force or fraud is contrary to one's long-term interests—despite the fact that one clearly benefits by taking into account today the consequences for tomorrow—any rational, future-oriented perspective is perversely categorized as self-sacrificial.

Morality's crucial concepts now have no clear definitions, only murky connotations—connotations that subvert the true meanings. "Selfishness," instead of denoting a concern for one's own interests (with the task of identifying the *nature* of self-interest belonging to the science of ethics), is vaguely associated with barbarians and con men. "Sacrifice," instead of denoting the surrender of a value for a non-value, is linked with a willingness to forgo instant gratification. "Altruism," instead of denoting the subordination of oneself to others, loosely suggests love and respect. This, sadly, is the intellectual muddle that makes people so vulnerable to the tyranny of need.

To the crucial question of why supporting your own life is supposedly not moral while supporting someone else's is, the philosophy of altruism offers no answer—not even a false one. In place of an explanation, the altruists simply invoke their straw man. They use the predator as a stand-in for selfishness, thereby evading the need to address the question of why *actual* selfishness is wrong.

But if we do address that question, and we penetrate the fog surrounding our moral concepts, it becomes clear that there is nothing to justify the call for self-sacrifice. Just as there is no earthly validation for physical enslavement, there is none for moral enslavement. There is simply nothing to warrant the notion that you exist to serve others. Your life is your own—and another person's need cannot give him a claim to it.

If there is nothing in reason on which to base altruism, what then is left? *Unreason.* The assertion that you must live for the sake of others—like the mystical assertion about an afterlife or about water being transformed into wine—relies not on facts and logic, but on the opposite: blind faith.

Auguste Comte, the nineteenth-century philosopher who coined the term "altruism," and who fully understood its meaning, aptly called it the "religion of humanity." He explained his basic approach to ethics: "It is henceforth a fundamental doctrine . . . that

the Heart preponderates over the Intellect."[7] Regarding his philosophy, he said, "the very principle on which its claim to universality
rests must be derived from Feeling."[8]

That is, to adopt altruism we must be led not by reason, but by
emotion. We must arrive at a moral conclusion not by validating it,
but by feeling it—not by knowing, but by believing—not because it
makes sense, but in spite of the fact that it doesn't.

The altruist doctrine tries to short-circuit the faculty of reason.
When people are drawn to believe that by acting for their own benefit they are emulating Attila the Hun—when they are continually
offered the false alternative of living parasitically off others or having
others live parasitically off them, when the nebulous definitions they
are given make self-interest seem repugnant and ineffectual while
self-renunciation seems praiseworthy and practical—they become
cognitively crippled in this area. They regard the entire sphere of
morality as inaccessible to the mind. In helpless resignation, they decide there is no rational means of discovering or practicing a proper
code of ethics.

The preachers of altruism, having induced this state of confusion, then cash in on it. Don't try to understand morality, they say.
Moral truths come not from the mind, but from the heart. Reason
is impotent. Don't look for explanations, just have faith. In what? In
society's demand that you subjugate yourself to the needs of others.

The code of altruism does not merely lack a logical answer to
why one should sacrifice: it rejects the *necessity* for such an answer. If
the recognized authorities proclaim that virtue consists of sacrifice,

you are instructed not to challenge them. Comte hailed Christianity's "submission of reason to faith," which, he said, "reduces to the subordination of man to Humanity."[9] In other words, you must simply will yourself to believe in the rightness of self-sacrifice. You are supposed to accept it in an act of sheer, unquestioning obedience.

The altruist creed, when stripped of its masks, rests on nothing else.

THREE

MORAL PRINCIPLES—
AND THEIR ENEMY

ALTRUISM DOES MORE THAN SIMPLY CONDEMN ACTS OF
selfishness: it severs egoism from the entire realm of ethics.

Once we understand why selfishness rests on reason, not wanton emotionalism, we need to examine the relation between self-
interest and a code of morality. Altruists claim that the pursuit of
self-interest, being a purely practical concern, requires no moral
guidance. Consequently, they say, the egoist can have only disdain
for moral principles. They want us to believe that the very purpose of
morality—not of any particular code, but of morality *as such*—is to
provide a prescription for selflessness. To them, altruism is not a certain theory of ethics, but is *synonymous* with ethics. To them, a moral
principle that conflicts with altruism is inconceivable.

Principles such as honesty, justice, integrity—the altruist insists—are definable, and defensible, only in terms of self-sacrifice. Honesty, for example, allegedly consists in forgoing self-interest by being truthful to others rather than profitably lying; justice, in forgoing self-interest by giving others what they deserve rather than the very least one can get away with; integrity, in forgoing self-interest by remaining loyal to what is right rather than by doing what is pragmatically expedient. But for the person who chooses to live for his own sake, such principles have no function according to altruism.

Yet in reality the reverse is true: it is the doctrine of egoism that makes moral principles an inescapable necessity.

THE SELFISH NEED FOR PRINCIPLES

Since life is conditional, "Do anything you wish" is not a formula for success. Reality imposes certain demands on us, the most fundamental of which is entailed in the Law of Identity. As the school of Aristotle put it: A is A—a thing is what it is. Everything has a specific nature. Oxygen allows our lungs to operate, carbon monoxide does not; food satisfies our nutritional needs, dirt does not; vaccines protect us against polio, voodoo does not. The Law of Identity requires us to acknowledge facts as facts, if we want to live. The irrational—the attempt to deny facts, the desire to flout reality—is destructive of life.

And life, for man, is lived not just in the here-and-now. It is in your interest, say, to drink when you are hot and thirsty. But your interest is obviously *not* served if you know the cold lemonade you are swallowing is laced with cyanide. The pleasure you derive in the first minute is worthless if it means dying in the second. The same is true if the effects of a decision materialize in the next year or the next decade. If you acknowledge only the present satisfaction you get from smoking two packs of cigarettes daily and evade the future harm your behavior invites, you are acting against your interests. Life is not a succession of discrete, splintered experiences. Sustaining your life means the *whole* of your life, not some isolated fragment of it. The entire issue of benefit and harm arises from your basic choice to live—and the choice to live is the choice to live beyond the immediate moment.

In the previous chapter I noted that selfishness calls for a long-range orientation. Now we can examine how this orientation is a crucial constituent of a morally principled life. To live we must take actions whose *total* consequences are in accord with reality. In any area, from diet to investments to career to sex, indulging an impulse of the moment, in disregard of the future, is detrimental. We therefore have to consider the ramifications of our decisions across our lifetimes.

That is, we must integrate today with all our tomorrows. We can allow no contradictions between them. We do not know every concrete causal sequence that will play out in the future, but we do know the one causal factor that is always present: the absolutism of reality. Reality does not disappear if we shut our eyes. If living is our goal, we have to keep our eyes—or, rather, our minds—in full focus.

What we need is not omniscience, but simply a willingness to know what can and should be known. We need a policy of long-term adherence to reality—a policy of not rationalizing, of not distorting, of not blanking out any facts—a policy, that is, of accepting the truth, the *whole* truth, unconditionally.

Proper moral principles provide us with that policy.

Honesty, for instance, is the principle that you should seek your values within the real world, not try to enter a counterfeit domain outside it. It is the principle that you should live with and by the facts, because trying to achieve your goals by faking reality is self-defeating. Honesty is not a command to sacrifice yourself, but the opposite: a prescription for *attaining* your self-interest. It is the recognition that the truth is the truth, regardless of anyone's attempt to circumvent it. It is the recognition that if you place yourself in conflict with reality, you are engaging in a war you must lose.

If a husband cheats on his wife, he is constructing a phony world not only around his deceived victim, but around *himself*. The truth becomes a danger to him, which he must keep trying to avoid. He must worry about any fact that might reveal his duplicity. And since all facts are connected in some way, every fact is a potential threat to him—a threat that keeps growing, as each lie inevitably requires others. If his wife discovers some fact that clashes with his pretenses, he must concoct further falsehoods to explain it away. Anyone who might cast doubt on his stories must be feared. Anyone who has seen him acting amorously toward his secret lover, from a hotel maid to a jewelry-store clerk, must be avoided. Does he want to introduce his wife to one of his co-workers? He can't—he told her he was working late at the office last night, and his colleague might contradict his story. Does he want to take her to a restaurant he likes? He can't— the maître d' remembers his candlelit dinner there with his paramour. Like a rudderless ship caught in a minefield, he flounders in a sea of lies, trying desperately to keep from colliding with the truth.

His fabrications lead to continual contradictions. He wants his wife's affection, yet the person to whom she grants it is not the person he has now become. He wants to maintain the marriage, but the relationship he wants it to represent is non-existent, and all that is left is a façade. He wants to be regarded by his friends as a respectable, trustworthy person, but the object of their evaluations is an illusion. By his dishonesty he has destroyed his own genuine values.

Life requires acting within reality; the adulterer makes himself live in an *un*reality. Life requires distinguishing between what is real and what is not; he obliterates that demarcation. He does not declare: "I accept the consequences of my decision to have an affair, I accept that I've chosen a different woman to be with, I accept that this means my marriage is over, I accept facts as facts." Instead, he evades the nature of his actions. He pretends that facts are non-facts, as he tries to eat his cake at home and have it on the side, too.

He is no different from the common thief, who rejects the constraints of reality by taking money that is not his. The thief blinds himself to the fact that everyone's life, including his own, depends on the principle that an individual's property is exclusively his and that no one may take it without the owner's consent. The thief has to pretend to himself that he is entitled to the money he seizes, just as the cheating husband has to pretend that he is entitled to whatever response he fraudulently wrests from his wife and his friends. Whether stealing goods or stealing affection, the perpetrator must pile lie upon lie in an effort to hide from the relentless truth. But since nothing other than the truth exists, there is nothing real that will give the dishonest person the sanctuary he seeks. Reality as such becomes his enemy.

A pianist who secures a concert engagement at the price of amputating his fingers, like the person who quenches his thirst by drinking lemonade he knows is poisoned, is not achieving a value—he is destroying that which makes the value possible. The same causal relationship exists in any dishonest attempt to gain a value. Human life depends on one's willing adherence to the demands of reality, which every act of dishonesty contradicts and undermines. Faking reality is like amputating the primary organ required for survival: one's mind. The faker is saying, in effect: "I am incapable of achieving my values—love, marriage, friendship, wealth—in the real world and must fabricate a different world. I must make myself dependent upon the distorted perceptions of dupes. I can succeed, not by perceiving and mastering reality, but only by trying to deny and escape it." But by saying: "I can't live in the real world," he is saying: "I can't live."

Honesty is man's indispensable tool for living in reality.

And the same function is served by all valid moral principles. Justice, for example, entails judging people according to what they *are*—what they are in reality, not in your fantasies. Justice requires treating a hero with admiration and a villain with contempt. It is in your interest that a productive genius be rewarded and encouraged, rather than resented for his abilities and penalized for his accomplishments. It is in your interest that a convicted pedophile be punished and shunned, rather than forgiven and hired as a kindergarten teacher. It is in your interest to judge everyone by an objective standard that distinguishes good from evil—i.e., that distinguishes a value from a threat.

Injustice is the pretense that someone is what he isn't. If law students cannot pass the bar exam or if business majors cannot do arithmetic, it is unjust, and contrary to your interest, for you to treat them the same as those who can. Any denial of reality in judging people—including the refusal to judge at all, for fear of being "judgmental"—is detrimental to your life.

Or consider the principle of integrity. Integrity is loyalty to your convictions, i.e., loyalty to your grasp of the truth. And your grasp of the truth is your means of dealing with reality. Standing firmly by what you know, rather than abandoning your views because others disapprove, is not quixotic but hard-headed and practical. If you are an atheist, can it be in your interest to pretend to be religious, thereby giving credence to an idea you regard as false and injurious, in order to appease your in-laws? If you are convinced that an unpopular political candidate deserves to be elected, can it be in your interest to campaign for his opponent in order to avoid the frowns of your neighbors? Denying the truth does not change it. It does not change the facts upon which you based your conclusion, and it does not change the fact that you know what you know.

All the moral principles of egoism call for fidelity to truth.* They demand that we place no consideration above reality, which means: no consideration above the judgment of our reasoning minds. Moral principles, in other words, demand rationality. As John Galt, the hero of Rand's novel *Atlas Shrugged*, puts it:

> A rational process is a *moral* process. You may make an error at any step of it, with nothing to protect you but your own severity, or you may try to cheat, to fake the evidence and evade the effort of the quest—but if devotion to truth is the hallmark of morality, then there is no greater, nobler, more heroic form of devotion than the act of a man who assumes the responsibility of thinking.[1]

This "responsibility of thinking" is the commitment to being guided, not by what you happen to feel, but by what *is*. It entails the understanding that emotions are not tools of cognition, that they do not tell you what is *in fact* good for you and that the requirements of life and happiness must be discovered by a purposeful act of thought. Rationality, because it is the primary necessity for living, is man's primary virtue. To be immoral is to be irrational—and to court self-destruction.

---

* For a full discussion of these principles, see Ayn Rand's "The Objectivist Ethics" in *The Virtue of Selfishness*.

The existential effects of violating a moral principle may not appear immediately. But the sheer choice to engage in a reality-flouting policy is already harmful, because it short-circuits the life-sustaining function of the mind. It erects a barrier between one's consciousness and reality. Playing Russian roulette is anti-life, even when the gun happens not to fire. It is a person's attempt to bypass reality—to wipe out awareness of the danger, to chase the "thrill" of thumbing his nose at reality, to convince himself that he can exist outside the boundaries of the rational. Such an attempt can be undertaken only by shutting one's mind to future consequences. But since there *are* future consequences, whether acknowledged or not, the very decision to ignore the facts places the evader on a road to doom. Whether he travels that road quickly or slowly, it leads to the same fatal destination. Whether disaster comes with the next spin of the revolver or in the wake of some other reality-defying whim, the policy he has chosen is a policy inimical to life.

THE MORAL *IS* THE PRACTICAL

Some may be taken aback by the idea that moral principles are practical. After all, we are regularly taught that the moral and the practical are incongruous, and that to choose one is to give up the other. But the source of this pernicious dichotomy is altruism. It is the code of altruism which maintains that to be moral is to sacrifice your interests. It is altruism that defines self-interest—the practical—as evil. According to the opposite code, however, there is no clash between the moral and the practical. Both rest on the same standard: the life of man *qua* rational being.

Man survives by means of reason—and embracing reason *means* embracing principles. To exercise the faculty of reason is, in essence, to see beyond what is immediately observed. It is to be aware not just of some concrete fact, but of how it relates to other facts one knows. It is to be aware not just of what is here now, but of what must have come before and what must come after. To use reason is to make inferences, identify similarities, discover connections, draw conclusions. It is to integrate all the facts into an ever-expanding, unified body of knowledge.

Thinking in principles, in any field, entails taking the widest perspective. It requires looking at the total context, i.e., at the big picture, not at a fleeting snapshot. It requires dealing with particular entities or events or experiences by relating them to broader truths. It requires a mind that is active, not compartmentalized. It requires that no phenomenon be treated as *sui generis*—as an isolated datum, incapable of being integrated with anything else. It requires a method of uniting narrow facts into explanatory generalizations, a method through which, instead of staring myopically at an apple falling or at the tide moving, you are able to grasp the far-reaching principle of gravity at work.

And when you apply this method to the field of morality, you grasp the broad fundamentals of human values. You bring a conceptual approach to the task of living. Instead of passively observing man's choices, instead of perceiving each concrete action in a vacuum, you integrate your observations into wider truths. You identify the essential nature of, say, honesty by recognizing the crucial similarity among *all* acts of honesty and by realizing how they advance your life, and how acts of *dis*honesty achieve the opposite. By not restricting your focus to the instantly perceivable, you discover the long-term effects of entire categories of action. You comprehend the causal principle that any attempt to deny reality is harmful to human life. You thereby understand, and seek to attain, the basic values required to sustain your existence across your lifespan.

A man of reason is a man who, in matters of cognition, *thinks* in principles and, in matters of ethics, *acts* on principles.

The unprincipled individual, however, rejects this perspective. He shrinks his intellect. Unlike the man of principle, who takes into account both the short- and long-term effects of his choices, he focuses on nothing but the immediate moment. The drug addict, the obsessive gambler, the inveterate playboy, the career criminal—these are all examples of this mentality. These are all types who are unwilling to integrate their current actions with future effects. They are not ignorant, but willfully blind. They refuse to see where their choices will lead.

To live an unprincipled life is to be driven by haphazard impulses and chance outcomes. It is a declaration that one will do whatever one feels like doing, and the facts be damned. The decision to repudiate moral principles is equivalent to the decision to play perpetual Russian roulette. They are both deadly in the long run—which is the critical time frame relevant to human life.

In sum, a principled dedication to truth is a *selfish* necessity—which explains why altruism must oppose it.

According to altruism, if something benefits you, you must give it away to others. While claiming to support moral principles, the altruist in fact holds that they too must be sacrificed on the altar of need. If you ask whether you should be honest, the altruist will answer: not if it hurts others, not if lying spares someone's feelings, not if your dishonesty satisfies another's needs.

Does the altruist believe that you should act with integrity? Not if doing so conflicts with the needs of others. For example, in the scene cited earlier from *The Fountainhead*, Howard Roark would be told to abandon his standards and to allow that ancient Greek façade to be patched onto his modern building, since compromise is what others need from him.

Should you be just? To the contrary, altruism insists that you treat people with mercy, rather than justice. If others are guilty of some wrongdoing, you should offer them absolution, not judgment. Treat them with pity in place of censure. Deal with people based not on what they deserve but on what they *need*.

Altruism's attitude toward moral principles is sharply illustrated by the following story. Some years ago, the campus of New York's Stony Brook State University became the target of numerous fires, resulting in several million dollars of damage. It turned out that the fires were set by one of the university's own fire marshals—who had previously been imprisoned for *arson*. While it is not clear whether anyone at the school knew of his criminal record at the time he was

MORAL PRINCIPLES—AND THEIR ENEMY

hired—he supposedly left blank the line on the application form that asked about criminal history—the university's chief fire marshal said such knowledge would have made no difference in the hiring decision: "We couldn't refuse him; that would be discrimination."[2] That is, it would have been unaltruistic for the university to be concerned about its own interest in keeping students and faculty safe from dangerous felons. It would have been unaltruistic to treat a criminal as a criminal, since the paramount consideration is supposed to be, not his character, but his acute need for the job.

An even more egregious example occurred at the Honeywell Corporation in Minnesota. There, an employee strangled to death a co-worker, his girlfriend, and was sent to prison for four-and-a-half years. Several weeks after his release, the company took him back—only to have him murder another co-worker, who was spurning his romantic overtures. Explaining the decision to re-employ him, a Honeywell spokesman said: "The philosophy we have is that we don't discriminate when it comes to hiring practices."[3]

It is true that employers may fear being sued for illegal discrimination if they reject such applicants. But the legal constraints themselves are simply the manifestation of altruism, of its mandate that we sacrifice everything, including our moral principles, for the sake of someone in need. Altruism demands that employers act dishonestly by hiding, from those who have a right to know, the dangerous background of the person being hired to work with them. It demands that employers suspend justice by treating as trustworthy someone who has demonstrated he isn't. It demands that employers violate their integrity by evading the knowledge that they are placing innocent people in jeopardy.

The same dismissal of moral principle is conveyed in the Biblical tale of Abraham, in which he stands ready to slaughter his son Isaac as a sacrificial offering to God. Instead of being regarded as a monster, for the horrific evil of trying to take the life of his own child simply because he was told to, Abraham is revered for his self-abnegating willingness to surrender something he treasures. Whether invoked in the name of God or in the name of the poor, the imperative of self-sacrifice is intended to supplant all moral considerations.

For an even more graphic illustration of the nature of this imperative, consider the case of Zell Kravinsky, a one-time multi-millionaire who took altruism very seriously.

After acquiring a $45 million fortune in real estate, Kravinsky gave almost all of it to charity. As a friend explained, "He decided the purpose of his life was to give away things." Still feeling unsatisfied, Kravinsky searched for a further opportunity to make sacrifices. He soon found one—he chose to donate a kidney to a total stranger. He provided this rationale: "The reasons for giving a little are the reasons for giving a lot. And the reasons for giving a lot are the reasons for giving more."[4]

His wife vehemently opposed his decision, arguing not only that he was in poor health, but that any of their four children might someday need a transplanted kidney from their father. However, as Abraham did not shrink from sacrificing his offspring, neither did

Kravinsky. "I love my children," he declared. "I really do. But I just can't say their lives are more valuable than any other life."[5]

Here we see the altruist's perverse concept of love put into practice. Kravinsky is talking about *his* children, but since it would be selfish for him to value them above others, he doesn't. Since authentic love, like any form of valuing, must be discriminating, altruism prohibits it. Just as altruism does not permit the employer to discriminate between a criminal and a non-criminal, so it does not permit a father to discriminate between his child and any other. Clearly, though, if a parent does not deem his own children more important to him than any other children, he does *not* love them. To "love" everyone equally is to be equally indifferent to all. Yet such appalling indifference is what Zell Kravinsky endorses.

Kravinsky underwent the risky surgery to remove his kidney strictly as an act of altruism. He dutifully cut away a piece of his life, because he believed that others had a higher claim to it.

It does not matter whether or not Kravinsky was prompted by some neurotic urge. (He made sure to inform the local news media the day of his kidney donation, saying: "I didn't expect to get the publicity, but I won't deny that it feeds my vanity."[6]) The crucial point is that, regardless of his actual motive, he did exactly what a paragon of altruism would do. His behavior was fully in accord with our culture's code of self-sacrifice.

Or, actually, not quite fully yet . . .

After the operation, Kravinsky expressed a desire to make a far greater sacrifice: giving away his other kidney—and more. "My organs could save several people if I gave my whole body away," he said. "I know it's a thing I ought to do; other lives are equal to my own, and I could save at least three or four."[7]

He wanted to become fodder for humanity. If someone needed a kidney, a lung, a cornea, a heart—Kravinsky would offer his, because he believed that the moral justification of an individual's existence is service to others. "I should just give all of me to those who need me, whether it is my body, my money or myself," he declared.[8]

While civilized society normally shrinks in horror and disgust at stories of cannibalistic tribes who kill their victims in order to eat their flesh, a different view prevails toward the modern version of the same abomination. For here is someone telling us that we ought to offer up our life-preserving body parts for consumption by others—yet no one publicly expressed any moral revulsion. To the contrary, Kravinsky was honored by the Pennsylvania General Assembly for being "a shining example of humanity."[9]*

Kravinsky may have offered his organs voluntarily, but what difference should that make? Whether the act is initiated by the eaters or by the eaten, it remains cannibalism—and it represents the essence of altruism. Whether others are hungry for all your flesh, or desire only your kidneys or merely ask you to pay for their food stamps, your altruistic duty is clear: since you have something they don't, you must be willing to sacrifice. In the man-eat-man world

---

* As a sign of the widespread admiration for Kravinsky's actions, there was even a planned movie of his life, starring noted actor Ralph Fiennes, which went through early stages of production.

decreed by altruism, the "have-nots" are granted an insuperable claim on anything you possess. As Kravinsky succinctly summed up the issue: "No one should have a vacation home until everyone has a place to live. No one should have a second car until everyone has one. And no one should have two kidneys until everyone has one."[10]

Need—the altruist asserts—overrides everything.

ALTRUISM AND THE ABSOLUTISM OF YOUR NEIGHBOR'S WISHES

Under the code of egoism, the good is determined by what is objectively necessary for sustaining man's life. The good does not consist in capriciously snatching an instant of mindless gratification. To act properly, you must know in principle what self-interest actually requires. The Russian-roulette player may tell himself he is acting selfishly, but he has in fact renounced the two absolutes on which the achievement of self-interest rests: reason and reality.

By an egoistic standard, if you experience an irrational desire, you should not accommodate it; saying no to such an emotion is an act of self-interest. But by an altruistic standard, if your neighbor expresses an irrational desire, you *should* accommodate it; saying no would be selfish on your part. If you encounter a homeless man panhandling for his next drug fix, you have no moral right to refuse him. It is selfish of you to withhold aid—and even more selfish to tell him that what he really needs is to stop using drugs and find gainful employment. Who are you to be so self-centered as to judge what other people really need? Who are you to reject a supplicant merely because you believe he does not deserve your assistance? Altruism does not permit such arrogant presumptuousness.

And neither does contemporary law. Thus, for example, an obese aerobics instructor in San Francisco, upon having her bid for a health-club franchise rejected by the franchisor for obvious reasons, files a successful complaint with the Human Rights Commission, arguing that city law forbids discrimination on the basis of weight.[11] Doctors with a history of drug addiction or mental illness are assured by the Justice Department that a medical board may not question them about their pasts, since such inquiries would cause doctors to be "singled out because of their disabilities."[12] A 640-pound contractor, recognized by the state of Maryland as a member of the minority class of corpulents, sues the city of Baltimore in order to receive preferential treatment in the awarding of municipal contracts.[13]

If people believe they have unmet needs, you are legally required to meet them. You may not insist that a person's actual interests are not advanced by irrational means—by coercion, by fraud, by injustice. You may not tell the needy that what they truly need is the opposite: a system in which individual rights are respected, force and deception are outlawed and justice is upheld. You may not admonish them to live off their own efforts rather than mooch off the work of others. You may not tell them they are harming themselves by seeking the unearned. If they believe they are entitled to your sacrifices, it is selfish of you to value your judgment over theirs.

To serve others means to provide what they lack, regardless of the nature and cause of that lack. To serve others means to satisfy their desires, whatever they are. The primacy of need, in other words, translates into: the primacy of the *wish*.

This premise is incompatible with a commitment to moral principles.

To adopt a moral principle is to identify something as good or bad, and to be directed by that fact, irrespective of anyone's wishes or feelings. A moral principle offers us conceptual guidance. It informs us that we should act in a certain manner, as against simply doing whatever we happen to feel like doing. It tells us that our behavior should be governed by firm precepts rather than by random, transitory impulses. A principle that declares something to be evil does not come with the qualifier: " . . . unless of course you really have an urge to do it." A moral principle does not tell us, say, that cannibalism is wrong unless we happen to feel hungry at the time. Instead, it provides us with a truth and instructs us to abide by it.

The elevation of emotion over reason, therefore, is the repudiation of moral principles.

Attila, the thorough emotionalist, is the paradigm of amoralism. Yet, like him, the altruist is led not by fixed principles but by unconstrained feelings. In keeping with Auguste Comte's pronouncement that "the heart preponderates over the intellect," altruism proclaims that everything must be subordinated to emotions. The basic difference between the Attila-ist and the altruist lies in the choice of whose emotions are paramount: yours or your neighbor's. While

Attila cheats, robs and kills when he feels it is good for *him,* the altruist instructs you to cheat, rob and kill when people in need feel it is good for *them.* The doctrine of altruism tells a school to cheat capable students out of a meaningful diploma, so that the needs of the incapable ones can be met; it tells an administrator to rob a university of its property by enabling a needy arsonist to burn down its buildings; it tells an employer to hire a convicted killer, and place all his workers at deadly risk, because the killer needs the job.

So while egoism is smeared as the unbridled indulgence of arbitrary desires, it is actually altruism that advocates such behavior, as long as those desires emanate from a non-you. And if being led by your own whims is a negation of moral principle, then so is being led by the whims of your fellow-man.

But—some may ask—what about altruism's devotion to mercy, to compassion, to humility? Doesn't that indicate a commitment to principles? No, it doesn't—not when moral principles are understood to mean allegiance to the truth.

The altruist, instead of judging people for what they actually are, believes in granting them mercy, which is based on what they aren't. Absolve the guilty, he says. Deny the reality of their actions and ignore the reality of their character. Treat them as though they were not guilty. Give them the forgiveness they need—that is, the forgiveness they *desire.*

Instead of being bound by the facts, the altruist believes in compassion. Feel sorry for people, he says. But which people? Should it be for those who want to live by the truth—the people who recognize the fact that an arsonist hired as a fire marshal, or a blind passenger seated in an exit row, poses a threat to the innocent? No, the compassion you are supposed to exhibit is toward those who want you to *distort* reality for their sake, toward those who want you to abet their wrongdoing, toward those who want you to renounce honesty in consideration of their feelings.

Instead of endorsing an uncompromising loyalty to one's convictions, the altruist believes in humility. Be self-effacing, he says. Be self-doubtful. Don't cling to what you know is right. Who are you to be so self-assured? Humble yourself. Sacrifice your certainty, i.e., sacrifice your integrity. Defer to the wishes of others—the wishes of those you know are wrong.

It is only under a code of rational egoism that facts, not feelings, constitute the foundation of ethics. It is only under egoism that actions are deemed right or wrong according to whether they meet an objective standard, not whether they satisfy someone's desires.

RATIONAL EGOISM PRECLUDES
CONFLICTS OF INTEREST

A system that converts wishes into entitlements, and which thereby has one rule for those who must be served and another for those doing the serving, makes conflict inescapable. If need is the standard and "no one should have two kidneys until everyone has one," there can be no amicable coexistence among people. Their lives will invariably clash.

The ethics of selfishness precludes such conflicts. Under egoism, there are no masters and no servants. There is one immutable principle, which applies to all: each man's life is an end in itself. Each individual is an autonomous being, with a fundamental right to his own existence. His moral purpose is not to serve others' needs but to pursue his own happiness.

Those who live by this code enjoy a harmony of interests. They do not seek the unearned, so there are no demands for sacrifice. They understand the selfish function of moral principles, so they live by the virtues entailed in a morality of rational self-interest. They respect the rights of others, because they realize that their own lives depend on the inviolateness of rights. Contrary to the altruist's man-as-beast premise, they do not go after their goals in the manner of hyenas drawn to a carcass, with each one's supper coming at the price of another's hunger. Since man lives by the mind, he does not, and cannot, survive as animals do. He does not live as a scavenger, but as a producer, of wealth. In the human world, life is not a zero-sum activity. Each individual creates the values he requires. And he deals with others, not by mooching or by looting, but by trading. Whether the relationship involves material or spiritual considerations, people offer value for value, to mutual benefit.

The magnificent prosperity we enjoy in the West testifies to this harmony of interests. Virtually every piece of wealth in our possession comes from the exchange of one person's productive work for another's. When bread is bought from a baker or a house is bought from a real-estate developer, when wages are received by a day laborer or dividends are received by a stockholder, self-interest motivates all participants in the transaction and makes each of them richer.

When people do disagree, they realize that the means of furthering their interests is reason, not its antipode: force. They grasp the principle that each person requires the freedom to live by the judgment of his mind rather than by the dictates of a gun. They understand that to sustain his life the individual must be able to keep the products of his thought and effort. They comprehend that whenever people deal with one another, it must be by common consent; and if no accord can be reached, everyone simply goes his separate way, with each acknowledging the other's unequivocal right to do so. (Of course, should any party choose to resort to force, he will be stopped by the law.)

The principles of selfishness encourage genuine goodwill among members of society. When one man's gain does not come at another's loss, and when people are not bound to each other by altruism's shackles, they can regard one another as potential values, not potential leeches. This attitude extends even to situations in which no trade is involved. It is the person who knows he has no duty toward others who can exhibit a benevolent, non-sacrificial generosity toward them, by giving directions to a lost traveler, for example, or by helping a blind man cross the street. If an egoist chooses to assist a stranger who is suffering through no fault of his own, he does so because of the value represented by human beings—which springs from the primary value of the individual self.

I should add that in the event of an emergency the egoist may be willing to take exceptional efforts to help another person. If he came across a drowning child, for instance, he would—if he could swim well enough—jump in to save him. But an emergency is by nature something extraordinary and short-lived. Once the child is safe, the rescuer will not then scour the planet for more drowning children. Nor will he feel obligated to make this child his permanent ward, feeding him, housing him and putting him through college.

Among rational individuals, there are no conflicts of interest. They all act on the same basic principles. They understand the meaning of self-interest, and they hold onto the full context of knowledge from which that meaning derives. Even when people are competitors—as when two businesses vie for the same customer or two applicants vie for the same job—all parties know that the existence of competition is ultimately in their interest, and that one party does not win through the sacrifice of the other. For example, the job applicant realizes that it is in his interest that there *be* jobs available. And just as every participant in an auction knows that the auction exists only because it is open to more than one bidder, a job-seeker knows that the job is there because it is open to more than one applicant. He knows that a free, capitalist society enables an employer to choose among potential employees, just as it enables the job-seeker to have more than one potential employer. Under such a system, competition arises because every individual is free to try to obtain the best job available by demonstrating that he offers the best value to an employer. The only way to eliminate competition would be to eliminate this freedom, by granting government bureaucrats the power to dictate who gets what job. But placing the livelihoods of job-seekers at the mercy of the state is patently not in their interest.

It is in your interest that there be free competition. It is in your interest that jobs be won by those who merit them. And if someone out-competes you, he has not taken away anything that actually belonged to you—the job was never yours; all that *was* yours was the right to try to persuade the employer to hire you, a right that remains unbreached. Your competitor's gain is not achieved by making you worse off.

Some incompetent grocery-bagger may complain that his interests collide with those of the Fortune 500 CEOs, since he would like to hold such a position and he needs it more than they do. Or some dissolute slacker, who yearns for competition-free jobs that grow on trees, from which they can be effortlessly plucked, may grumble that his interests are being harmed by his having to fill out job applications and submit to interviews. But the whiners' dissatisfaction is misdirected. Their wish to live in some fantasy world—like any belief that one can seek a goal while being oblivious to the means required to attain it—is what conflicts with their actual interests. Self-interest can be identified only *within* the realm of existence, not outside it. Self-interest consists of the pursuit of values consonant with the demands of an unbending reality. It does not consist of arbitrary, self-contradictory whims. People may indulge in all sorts of irrational desires—desires that clash with reality—which lead them into all sorts of conflicts with others. But a conflict of wishes is *not* a conflict of interests.[14]

It is altruism, by replacing desert with need, that generates continual conflicts. And these conflicts are not just between one person and another, but within the soul of everyone who follows this doctrine, or *tries* to follow it. For no matter how much someone chooses to sacrifice, he will discover that it is never enough.

For example, Bill Gates has donated to charity a sum greater than the gross national product of each of more than one hundred nations. But he is far from satisfying the edicts of altruism. As philosopher Peter Singer maintains, in an article titled "What Should a Billionaire Give—and What Should You?":

> Gates may have given away nearly $30 billion, but that still leaves him sitting at the top of the *Forbes* list of the richest Americans, with $53 billion. His 66,000-square-foot high-tech lakeside estate near Seattle is reportedly worth more than $100 million. . . . Among his possessions is the Leicester Codex, the only handwritten book by Leonardo da Vinci still in private hands, for which he paid $30.8 million in 1994. Has Bill Gates done enough? More pointedly, you might ask: if he really believes that all lives have equal value, what is he doing living in such an expensive house and owning a Leonardo Codex? Are there no more lives that could be saved by living more modestly and adding the money thus saved to the amount he has already given?[15]

Based on the premise of altruism, this argument is unanswerable. If one has a duty to sacrifice for others, then Bill Gates is clearly in violation—and so is every other human being. As long as you are alive, you have something that can be sacrificed to others. Any value you enjoy is being kept from its rightful users: those who lack it. Every action you take in living your life amounts to theft from the needy. If you have a house, a car, a savings account, a pair of shoes, a functioning kidney—why are you not giving it away to others? Why are you living better than the most wretchedly miserable person on earth? Is it because you believe that your life belongs to *you*, not to anyone else? Only a morality of selfishness could justify such a view.

At root, the conflicts spawned by the doctrine of self-sacrifice stem from the opposition between the demands of altruism and the demands of human life. The two are antithetical. You cannot live while surrendering your life to others. If you accept altruism, you discover that there is no way to practice it consistently. Instead, your life becomes a series of hopeless oscillations between guilt-ridden acts of self-interest and teeth-gritting acts of self-sacrifice—between cynical amoralism and resentful martyrdom. According to the altruist morality, the very fact of your existence is cause for guilt. The very fact that you devote resources to sustaining your own life is evidence that you are in dereliction of your duty to sacrifice for others.

The code of altruism offers no guidance for the task of living. It is irrelevant to your *personal* concerns. It has no advice on how to *achieve* your values, only on how—if you do manage to achieve something—to give them away. The rational individual regards his life as precious and wants to know what he ought to do to live it, not to surrender it. He understands that his life depends on his making the right choices, and he wants to learn what they are. He wants to discover how to attain his long-range happiness. He wants to be guided by an objective concept of the good, which he can judge by means of reason, rather than by a concept that rests on faith and feelings. He wants, in other words, a set of principles to help him live successfully on earth.

He cannot get it from altruism.

FOUR

THE MYTH OF THE "PUBLIC INTEREST"

SELF-SACRIFICE IS THE ANTITHESIS OF SELF-INTEREST. What one sacrifices, obviously, are one's interests. But the proponents of altruism want to obscure this fact. Toward that end, they promote the notion of the "public interest"*—a term with no clear definition, but with one unmistakable function: to make altruism seem practical. They aim to instill in us the vague sense that it is to our advantage to serve others, when those others are the so-called public. They want us to believe that since we are all part of society, we all benefit in some way by making sacrifices in the name of the public interest.

---

* I generally place quotation marks around "public interest" (or "public good" or "public need") to indicate that it is a misleading term. For ease of reading, though, all future references to it in this chapter will omit the quotes; I rely on the reader to keep in mind my view of the invalidity of the term.

The effectiveness of this term, though, depends on our not inquiring too closely about its meaning.

It is never made clear exactly who is considered the public, how its interests are determined and over whom it is supposed to take precedence. The public interest is ordinarily differentiated from so-called private, or special, interests. It is widely assumed that the two types of interests clash, and that for a society to function, the public interest must be elevated above private ones. But how do we know which is which? We are typically told that something is in the public interest if it helps society as a whole, whereas private interests benefit a selfish few, and exclude everyone else.

A bromide, however, is not an explanation. How does one in fact judge what helps "society as a whole"?

WHO QUALIFIES AS THE PUBLIC?

If a piece of land is taken over by the city for use as a park, the public interest is said to be served; but if the land is bought to be used as a private shopping center, it isn't. Why? To reply that the public interest is served when public resources—i.e., resources controlled by government—are used, simply begs the question. The government exerts such control precisely because doing so supposedly furthers the public interest, while the private alternative does not. But why is a city-owned park a benefit to the public while a private shopping center is not? Why is a municipal library in the public

interest while a private movie theater is not? Why does constructing a national museum further the public interest but constructing a private parking garage does not? The customers of shopping
centers and movie theaters and parking garages undeniably benefit. They willingly patronize such facilities, over and over. And
if sheer numbers are the yardstick, which serves people's interests
better—Yellowstone Park, which has three million visitors a year,
or Disney World, which has forty-five million? The Bronx Zoo,
which attracts two million people annually, or Minnesota's Mall
of America, which draws forty million? Public television, which
averages a prime-time audience of under two million households,
or commercial television, which reaches over eighty million? By
what criteria is the public interest distinguished from a private interest? What, in other words, makes a person part of the public
when he visits Yellowstone, but part of the non-public when he
visits Disney?

The public interest is certainly not a mere euphemism for the
alleged interests of the poor. After all, the average visitor to Yellowstone is probably richer than the average visitor to Disney. Or look
at broadcasting. The reason behind the creation of public broadcasting is surely not poverty on the part of its audience, inasmuch
as commercial broadcasters require no monetary payment from the
viewer. (To say nothing of the fact that here too the viewers of the
public product are on average wealthier than those of the private
product.)

If neither the number nor the economic status of the beneficiaries is the critical factor, what then is? The *manner* in which they benefit. The essence of the public-private distinction is captured by a less murky alternative: alms versus trade.

When a profit-making entity charges people for what they use, the arrangement is typically dismissed as narrowly private. But when people get something for which they *don't* have to pay, a broad public good is ostensibly being served. A public-interest project is by nature non-commercial. Whether people use it for free or must make a nominal payment, the full cost is never covered by those who use it (if it were, the project would be commercially viable). The cost is not intended to be borne by the users. It is not intended to be borne by paying customers. That is, no *trade* is supposed to take place: the provider does not aim to profit, and the benefit each user receives is not in return for his payment. Instead, people are given "free" parks, "free" skating rinks, "free" concerts and "free" libraries because the public interest requires it—a public interest that could not be realized if people had to pay private owners for the very same things.

Someone, though, pays for these "free" goods. They do not materialize magically. They all have a cost—and it is shouldered by those who are being *harmed* by public-interest undertakings.

Under the standard of self-interest, each person pays for what he uses, because he pays for what he *values*. A Disney World, for instance, exists because each of its paying customers has decided that it offers him something worthwhile. The users of a given product judge that it warrants the cost, while those who disagree spend their money elsewhere, on something they value more. All parties benefit and no one's interest is sacrificed.

But under a public-interest standard, *non-users* pay. They are compelled, as taxpayers, to finance what is *not* a value to them, on the premise that they have a moral duty to provide for the public interest. The link between payer and beneficiary is sundered. Instead there are only those who must sacrifice and those for whom the sacrifice is made, as non-users pay without benefiting and users benefit without paying. *This* is the hallmark—and the central purpose—of a public-interest activity.

Of course, ascertaining whether any particular individual in fact benefits from such an activity is highly problematic. When the government determines that some project serves the public interest, its decision is enforced by law. Thus, while you might enjoy a stroll in a public park, you have no way of knowing how much you are actually paying, through a myriad of untraceable taxes and foreclosed opportunities, for that pleasure. You have no way of calculating whether the benefit *to you* is worth the cost *to you*. Indeed, the very point of any public-interest project is to make such assessments impossible—and irrelevant.

There are, however, two facts you *can* ascertain: first, that these government-backed projects would not exist if people were free to choose whether to pay for them; and second, that once they are brought into existence, they represent a net loss to all the payers—a loss of all the forgone goods and services on which they would have preferred to spend their own money.

The public-interest promoters are indifferent to anyone's actual preferences. They invoke the public interest as a justification not just for parks and zoos, but for every type of government intervention—that is, as a justification for negating the judgment made by individuals about their own interests.

For example, when politicians in New Jersey prohibit the operation of self-service gasoline stations, or when politicians in New York City compel every taxi driver to carry a global-positioning-system device, their explanation is that they are protecting the public interest. But this protection consists in overriding the decisions of all the people who prefer self-service stations and GPS-less taxicabs.

In the absence of government interference, producers and consumers determine the nature of a business. If there is sufficient demand—demand that businesses, unlike government, cannot afford to dismiss—some gasoline stations will offer self-service and others will offer full-service. If a particular station is self-service, it is because the people who make the station possible—the people willing to expend their effort and capital to build and operate it, and the people willing to spend their money to patronize it—prefer that option. Every government-mandated full-service station that would otherwise have been self-service is a nullification of those choices.

Similarly, in a free market some taxis will feature a GPS, to satisfy the customers who are willing to pay for it; other taxis won't, to satisfy the ones who are unwilling to pay for it. Everyone gets, not what he fantasizes about and not what he grumbles to his legislators about, but what he is *willing to pay for*. Supply matches demand: each party must meet the requirements of the other. Transactions occur only when the interests of both buyer and seller, as judged by each party, are fulfilled.

But altruism holds that self-interest must be banished as the basis for deciding what goods and services are available. So the public-interest spokesmen intercede, announcing that *they* will determine what the public wants. When the decree is issued requiring all gasoline stations to be full-service or requiring all taxis to carry a GPS, you are prevented from buying what someone is willing to sell you, or from selling what someone is willing to buy from you. You are made to surrender your interests to the interests of those deemed the public.

And who exactly is the public here? It is anyone who insists that he be provided with some product that is not being offered to him voluntarily. It is all those who, like an infant throwing a tantrum, demand that their wishes be accommodated because of the absolutism of their *need*. In other words, if you want to act on the basis of self-interest and obtain what you seek from others by trade, you must subordinate yourself to the public interest; if instead you want to obtain something through the sacrifice of others, then you *are* the public.

PUBLIC INTEREST: MAKING PEOPLE
PAY FOR WHAT THEY DON'T WANT

Since they interpret need as a lack that can be remedied only by another's sacrifice, altruists disdain trade. A commercial transaction, regardless of how many people willingly participate and how much they genuinely benefit, is not regarded as meeting real needs. If people leave Walmart with carfuls of merchandise, their needs have not been satisfied; they have simply traded their own money for the store's wares. If, however, they leave a public library with some books, then their needs *are* being met, because they are getting something for which they are not directly paying.

By opposing the value of trade, and of individual choice, the public-interest standard spawns goods and services that people would categorically reject in a free market. Here is how Connecticut Public Television (CPTV), in a fund-raising letter to viewers, lauds the public service it furnishes: "Imagine getting a few months of free service from the phone or electric company. Unfortunately, we live in a world where you pay as you go."

That is, because commercial firms function by offering their customers something valuable enough to pay for—a fact somehow considered "unfortunate"—those who fail to pay don't receive the service. If, however, CPTV tried the same arrangement with its customers, it would have no viable audience. How does it remedy this? By acting as though its inability to attract an authentic market for its product is a virtue—and by deciding, as the letter proceeds to explain, to exist on handouts: "Now, imagine a service that keeps coming to your home even if you ignore the bill for years. . . . CPTV lets you decide whether or not to 'pay your bill.' And, we let you decide how much to pay."[1]

Here is what CPTVs message really means: "We realize that our audience does not value our product enough to pay for all of our costs, even if part of the price is just spending time in front of a TV set. Nonetheless, we need money from you, so that we can continue to provide the public with the programming that, unfortunately, it largely ignores."

So the station gives away its product as alms, and pleads for alms in return. Consider the bizarre inversion this represents. Because a commercial broadcaster must draw a large audience in order to survive—because it profits only by delivering programs that its customers value—because it relies on advertising, which must *persuade* people that they will benefit by purchasing various products—it is scorned for advancing purely private interests. But when a broadcaster offers non-commercial programming, the distinctive characteristic of which is its *failure* to appeal to very many people—when it is subsidized by taxpayers, who would not voluntarily support the programming—when it scorns commercial advertising as crass and disruptive, but regularly subjects its audience to the interminable pleading of pledge-drives—then it is hailed as a guardian of the public interest.

Satisfying a public need, in broadcasting or in any other realm, means harming some people for the benefit of others. It means that some must pay so that others might have their desires indulged—whether the desire is for James Joyce on PBS, a sports stadium on city land, a federally subsidized airline in an isolated town or an orchestra in a state-sponsored theater. It does not matter, in any given instance, whether the few are sacrificed for the many or the many for the few. Alleviating need—i.e., fulfilling some people's wish to benefit without paying—is all that counts.

Accordingly, there is no way to define, or to delimit, the public interest. It is a label that can be applied at will, as long as there is any collection of people, large or small, with unmet needs.*

Political commentators regularly decry government boondoggles. When Washington subsidizes a blueberry-research center in Maine,[2] or underwrites a Hawaiian documentary on the Bushmen of the Kalahari Desert,[3] or funds the renovation of a shrine to Mother's Day in West Virginia,[4] or issues a grant to an Arizona scholar to translate Icelandic poetry[5] or launches a tattoo-removal program for gang members in California[6]—critics wonder how such measures ever came to be approved. They accuse government officials of callously disregarding the public interest.

But it is the boondoggle-approvers who are being loyal to the public interest, and the critics who are betraying it. Since the public is any group with unfulfilled needs, why shouldn't the recipients of these boondoggles be eligible? There are indeed people who *need* to have their tattoos removed—who wish, as the *New York Times* puts it, to "erase a social stigma"[7]—and want others to pay the costs. There

---

* Of course, a non-profit entity, if it is fully private, does not fall into this category. Such an organization is not providing some nebulous public service to the detriment of private interests. To the contrary, it is engaged in a trade, in an exchange of values between willing parties. It is advancing the particular interests of the particular individuals who voluntarily supply its funding.

are indeed people who *need* to tell the story of the long-ignored Kalahari Bushmen, or to demonstrate the allure of Icelandic poetry, or to communicate the importance of motherhood or to reveal the hidden potential of the blueberry, but want others to subsidize their desires. If we are to comply with the code of altruism, these needs have to be met.

As for the needs of the people who have to pay for all this—i.e., their need to spend their money on their own lives, in pursuit of their own goals—those are merely selfish, private interests, according to altruism, and deserve no moral consideration.

Whether the issue is prohibiting self-service gasoline stations, or establishing public parks or financing the removal of tattoos, the premise is the same: if some people have a desire the fulfillment of which comes at the expense of other people, a public interest is born. Since people need these things—or some government bureaucrat glibly asserts that they do—everyone else must sacrifice.

There is nothing practical about altruism, no matter how seductively it is dressed in public-interest garb. Self-sacrifice is the sacrifice of one's *self.* When you are urged to comply with the public interest, you are being told to act contrary to your self-interest. The public-interest tenet holds that the number of individuals who must suffer is immaterial, since the condition of society as a whole is being improved.

But there is no such thing as "society as a whole." The public is not some disembodied object. It is not a single, undifferentiated mass, existing apart from the individuals who comprise it. The public *is* those individuals. The assertion of a clash between public and private interests is meaningless. The clash is only between some individuals and other individuals, between the ones who wish to be given something without having to pay for it, and the ones who want to spend their own money for their own benefit. It is a conflict between the individuals who demand a sacrifice and those from whom they demand it.

If the proponents of the public interest looked at actual individuals, the nature of this conflict would be obvious. But they don't *want* to see individuals. To the contrary, they want to do away with the very idea of the individual. To embrace their amorphous, identityless public, they have to transform it into some unearthly entity, an entity that transcends individuals. That is, they have to adopt a philosophy of *collectivism*.

INDIVIDUALISM VS COLLECTIVISM

There are two principal approaches for assessing man in a social context. One is based on individualism, which regards the individual as the primary unit of mankind and which maintains that each person has an independent existence and a right to his own happiness. Accordingly, there is one fundamental fact, as well as one fundamental value, on which the moral-political structure rests: the life of the individual.

Collectivism takes the opposite approach.

Collectivism holds that the group is primary. Collectivism derives from altruism and is an extended mode of abnegating the self.

It is the view that the individual is metaphysically insignificant. It is the view that he is not an independent entity, but merely one of many interchangeable cells of the "social organism," and that he is only a means to that organism's ends. Accordingly, there is one fundamental fact, as well as one fundamental value, on which the moral-political structure rests: the existence of the group.

Under the individualist philosophy, sustaining your life entails *self*-generated action. The knowledge you acquire, the abilities you cultivate, the money you earn—all are the products of your efforts and rightfully belong to you. You can, of course, engage in cooperative activity with others, but whatever part of the total effort is yours, *is yours alone.*

Under the collectivist philosophy, life consists of *socially* generated action. Everything you achieve is attributable to, and is at the disposal of, the collective. Is your income, for example, the result of your efforts? Not according to the advocates of collectivism. You can be the most brilliant innovator and earn vast riches, but according to the co-director of the organization called Responsible Wealth: "It takes a village to raise a billionaire. Every taxpayer deserves some credit for 'Forbes 400' wealth."[8] You are thus deluding yourself if you think you have worked for your money. "Self-made wealth is a myth," declares the chairman of the political science department at Moravian College, since "[a]ll wealth originates in the community."[9] Using this premise, a Nobel Prize winner in economics endorses the confiscation of virtually all of everyone's earnings: "On moral grounds, then, we could argue for a flat income tax of

90 percent to return that wealth to its real owners"[10]—i.e., to the general public.

What about your brain? Are your ideas the product of your own thinking? Certainly not, say the collectivists—ideas arise from the anonymous masses. For instance, there is opposition to the existence of copyright, the intellectual deed held by the originator of a literary or artistic work, because its "emphasis on individual contribution and individual ownership takes precedence over the concept of 'community knowledge.'"[11] A *New York Times* editorial, in response to a proposal to lengthen the duration of copyrights, insists that "the public has an equally strong interest in . . . returning[!] works to the public domain—the great democratic seedbed of artistic creation—where they can be used without paying royalties."[12] So the mainspring, and the true owner, of all ideas is supposedly society as a whole, which then may or may not magnanimously grant an author the privilege of borrowing, and claiming credit for, its creations.

Do you believe that at least your *life* belongs to you? Collectivists disagree. Their position, perfectly expressed in a legal brief on assisted suicide, is that "life is a social duty" and that "the individual has an affirmative duty to continue living" because of an "implicit social compact." That is, "[t]o be a member of society, the person . . . must remain alive." Even when someone is suffering the agonies of an incurable, terminal disease, he has no right to end his own life. Suicide "is an intensely social act . . . amenable to social control, since it has a dramatic impact on others." It is an act "requiring the assent of society as a whole."[13] So you may not choose to take your life unless you receive public permission. The author of this brief quotes approvingly from an 1802 handbook of English criminal law: "The law regards [suicide] as an heinous offence . . . for as the public have a right to every man's assistance, he who voluntarily kills himself is with respect to the public as criminal as one who kills another."[14]

Just as under ancient monarchies the citizens were rightless subjects, readily expendable by the king if they failed to serve his needs—so in modern times we are, according to collectivist doctrine, serfs of society. Collectivists deny not just the individual's moral autonomy, but his essential existence. They view him as having no reality apart from the group—no reality except as one of many indistinguishable cogs enabling the collective machine to function—so that suicide and murder are equally objectionable, in that both diminish the resources of society.

When collectivists impel you to sacrifice your money, your ideas or your life for society, they don't acknowledge that you are being harmed for the sake of others. That perspective is alien to them. Rather, they see only a single, all-encompassing social body. They proclaim: "Let us have public parks and public schools and public housing, let us make available job-training advisors and social workers, let us offer unemployment insurance, universal health care and a guaranteed minimum income"—and they refuse to grasp the fact that particular human beings have to pay for these things. The frozen thought in their collectivized minds is only: "The public needs these things, and the public provides them."

This reification of society is the legacy of a long line of philosophic thought. Its main inspiration is the teachings of history's arch-collectivist: Hegel. Each of us is but a fragment of some mystical whole, according to this early nineteenth-century thinker. Hegel believed that the universe is suffused with a cosmic "Spirit," into which we must permit our inconsequential selves to be absorbed:

A single person, I need hardly say, is something subordinate, and as such he must dedicate himself to the ethical whole. Hence, if the state [i.e., the incarnation of the whole] claims life, the individual must surrender it.[15]

The state, Hegel says, "has supreme right against the individual, whose supreme duty is to be a member of the state."[16] The individual must aspire to become one with the cosmic collective. As explained by one of his scholarly interpreters, Hegel's view is that "the life of the whole appears in all of the parts. This means that the true life of the parts, i.e., the individuals, is found in and is identical with the life of the whole."[17]

These ideas may seem like the abstruse ramblings of an irrelevant, ivory-tower professor—but the essence of Hegel's philosophy shapes our social policies today. Social Security is a good illustration of a program firmly rooted in Hegelian soil. When money is taken from a working twenty-five-year-old, it is not saved for his own retirement in forty years. Despite the bookkeeping façade of individual accounts, everyone understands that all the funds go into one collective pot. No one in the Social Security system has funds put aside for his own future. Every dollar collected from workers is spent immediately on a group of current retirees. And when those workers retire, they will similarly have to rely not on their own saved earnings, but on the impounded earnings of the next batch of active workers.

The implicit premise behind this program is that there are no individual workers, but only transposable cells toiling away for the benefit of the social organism. It is in the public interest that some pay for others—and that no one pays for himself. The collective puts in and the collective takes out. This is how you are supposed to view the workings of the system. And this is why the system, heralded as improving the lives of all, allows no one the choice of whether to participate.

You may wish to leave the program. You may wish to take care of your own retirement needs by accumulating savings, so that your principal is preserved, allowing you to end up with more than Social Security would give you (even using the most conservative invest-ment strategy). But the system will not permit you to regard yourself as an end rather than a means. The system requires that each worker docilely submit to having his money taken away and redistributed on behalf of the public interest. The system cannot abide voluntary action. As an editorial in the *Washington Post* argues:

If Social Security were voluntary, it wouldn't be the rich who would opt out. . . . [M]any young people who find themselves hard-pressed to buy a home, educate children or help aging parents might choose to avoid the relatively large slice that payroll taxes take from moderate wages. In time they—and their children—would come to regret that choice.[18]

In other words, you cannot be allowed to plan your own life, since you just don't know what is best for you.

The denial of individual choice is central to the whole public-interest approach to politics. What is trumpeted as the public interest does not simply supersede your interests; it *constitutes* your interests, if only you understood them properly. And since you lack the necessary wisdom, the collectivists insist, the state must force you to act in a way that will ultimately lead you to happiness.

This too is straight out of Hegel, who says that in political matters "it is not the isolated will of individuals that prevails; individual pretensions are relinquished, and the *general will* is the essential bond of political union" (emphasis added).[19] The individual has no right to his own judgment; the will of the collective must direct his behavior. And how is that collective will to be ascertained? Do we take a poll, with the most popular view winning? No, that would retain vestiges of individualism, conceding to each voter the ability to judge. The populace, Hegel asserts, "does *not* know what it wills. To know what one wills . . . is the fruit of profound apprehension and insight, precisely the things which are *not* popular."[20]

Individuals, in this view, cannot know the truth—including the truth about their own interests. Only the collective, or its embodiment, the state, possesses the requisite "profound apprehen-sion and insight." Only when you sacrifice your own, narrow-minded interests, therefore, can you genuinely benefit. Only the "general will," as reflected in the decisions of government, is your *true* will, and only the mystical public interest represents your *true* interest. To choose not to participate in the Social Security system is thus a misguided decision, from which you have to be rescued. You must be compelled to participate so that your best interests can be realized. The benefits engendered by any product of individual, private choice—a 401(k) plan, a Disney World park, a FedEx delivery system, a Barnes & No-ble bookstore—are superficial. Only the products of a selfless "gen-eral will"—a Social Security program, a Yellowstone Park, a federal postal service, an Icelandic poem subsidized by the National Endow-ment for the Arts—can achieve our real interests. "[T]he state"—according to Hegel—"is the true self of the individual."[21]

THE PUBLIC INTEREST IS *NOT* WHAT INTERESTS THE PUBLIC

Putting this point in more contemporary terms is a former chairman of the Federal Communications Commission (FCC), in a speech to executives of the broadcast industry about what we should be al-lowed to watch on television:

> I am here to uphold and protect the public interest. . . . Some say the public interest is merely what interests the public. I disagree. . . .

[Y]our obligations are not satisfied if you look only to popularity as a test of what to broadcast. . . . It is not enough to cater to the nation's whim—you must also serve the nation's needs.[22]

Do audiences want certain programs? Irrelevant, the FCC says. People are unable to determine what is good for them. Their interests, as Hegel explains, consist of "precisely those things which are *not* popular"—i.e., they consist of what people do *not* want. They are whatever some spokesman for the collective will—in this case, the head of a regulatory agency—declares them to be. So your choice of what to watch on television is disdained by the FCC as a "whim." But when government bureaucrats dictate what you can watch, they are deemed to be making objective decisions that satisfy your real needs.

Another head of the FCC echoed this philosophy when he chastised two of the major networks for airing entertainment programs rather than a debate between presidential candidates:

Some argue that the networks are right to respond to the viewers who would much prefer watching almost anything other than the first presidential debate. . . . But as the trustees of the public airwaves, the networks must do more than just entertain: they must also serve the needs of citizens by facilitating an informed democratic process. . . . And in the future, the networks should remember that the public interest is far more important than their financial interest.[23]

Since the networks achieve their financial interest only by providing programming that people find of greatest value, the FCC obviously believes—in keeping with Hegelian doctrine—that the public interest requires giving people something they do *not* value, and that their true interests can be known only by the government.

Dictatorships typically hold sham elections, in which the outcome is predetermined. An official of the old Soviet Union once offered an illuminating justification for this practice: "We think the possibility of making a wrong choice is reduced because we make the choice before the election."[24] Can the apostles of the public interest disagree? Is there any difference between choosing your retirement plan, your television shows—or your political officeholders?

Because the goals pursued in the name of the public interest are not chosen by the affected individuals themselves, those goals are detached from any private, or *actual,* interests. There is no logical way for one man, after expropriating the money of another, to decide how best to spend that money in furthering the interests of his victim. This is doubly true when the expropriators are politicians, who must decide how "society as a whole" ought to have its money spent. Does the public want a refurbished ice skating rink or an additional wing for the library? A Little League baseball complex or an opera house? A new bridge or a new railroad station? Every individual, as a producer or as a consumer, decides all the time how to spend his money, based on his own hierarchy of values. These decisions determine which products are made available in the market and which aren't. But when the government is acting on behalf of the public interest, it is in effect telling people: "We're taking your money, which you would have spent on something else, and we're spending it on what we deem will better advance your interests." In that context, what rational basis can there be for selecting one option over another? The choices are entirely arbitrary.*

And one of the ugliest pieces of evidence for this arbitrariness is the proliferation of lobbying.

Hordes of pressure groups regularly descend upon government, seeking legislative and regulatory favors. How do they succeed? Their activities are not secret. The lobbyists' names, clients and objectives are publicly registered. They do not generally rely on outright bribery. To the contrary, they work within the law—the law that enshrines the public interest. They succeed precisely because they can appeal to, and hide behind, that fuzzy concept. Virtually every lobbyist maintains that his goals will benefit society. From global-positioning-system manufacturers eager to have their products installed in New York's taxicabs, to blueberry growers who want more people to enjoy their crop, to tattoo parlors ready to offer their services to "remove a social stigma," the argument is always that a public need is being filled. And by the criterion of collectivism, there is no way to refute this. Who on earth can explain whether the consumption of blueberries represents a special interest or a public interest?

---

* Obviously, this applies only to the areas in which individuals can and should make their own choices—that is, areas involving peaceful, voluntary dealings between people. But where physical force is involved, such as in the work of police, only government, not the private citizen, is entitled to act—as we will see in Chapter 5.

At root, it is not the politicians' venality, but the impossible subjectivity of the public interest, that allows lobbyists to wage their pressure-group warfare. A judge who must determine whether a defendant is innocent or guilty has a clear-cut standard by which to decide. But a politician who must determine whether a proposed law is or is not in the public interest, doesn't. There is no honest, objective way for him to make that decision. There is no honest, objective principle by which money can be taken away from some individuals and spent on behalf of those anointed as the public.

People normally understand that a thief is illegitimately lining his pockets when he loots his victim. It is the novel contribution of collectivism to justify such crime by contending that since both parties are interchangeable parts of the whole, the money is merely being transferred from one pocket of the public to the other.

THE COLLECTIVIST MENTALITY

Of course, the collectivists' goal is much more ambitious than the mere redistribution of income. Their deepest aim is to have you acknowledge the collective as the fundamental source of your identity. You are to regard yourself not as an individual, but only as a component—an inconsequential, pliant, easily replaceable component—of the collective.

In more primitive times, the tribe would select someone to be sacrificed to the gods—not because of anything he had done, but so that the tribe could hope for good fortune in exchange for offering up a part of itself. In today's times, you may be granted or denied admission to college—not because of anything you have done, but so that your race or gender can be rewarded or penalized. In both eras, individuals are being defined, not by their own attributes, but simply by membership in a group.

According to the ethics of altruism, you are not important; only the non-you is—and the biggest non-you is the collective. Altruism is the primacy of need, and collectivism is the primacy of the needs of the group. Give up self-responsibility, the collectivist says, and embrace group-responsibility. Abandon the autonomous self. Be dependent on the collective. Accept the authority of the group—of whatever group claims you as a constituent.

This collectivist mentality is inculcated in our classrooms, from kindergarten onward. Heavily influenced by the theories of Progressive education, schools believe that their central task is to instruct children, not in how to acquire knowledge, but in how to become "socialized." For several generations, our children have been trained to place the group above the individual. The father of Progressive education, John Dewey, proclaimed that "the school is primarily a social institution"[25] and that "the true center of . . . school subjects is not science, nor literature, nor history, nor geography, but the child's own social activities."[26] The child, he said, should be "stimulated to act as a member of a unity . . . and to conceive of himself from the standpoint of the welfare of the group to which he belongs."[27] Dewey insisted that the goal of education "is the development of a spirit of social cooperation and community life."[28] This is achieved in the child by "saturating him with the spirit of service."[29]

Dewey's ideas infuse our system of education. Children are taught that the individual is insignificant, and that no single student should stand out, or stand apart, from the others. One school's third-graders, for example, have all their private school supplies—pencils, paper, rulers, etc.—confiscated at the start of the semester and placed in a communal pool for all to use; this practice, according to the principal, serves to "teach kids to care about each other and appreciate the common good."[30]

Under Dewey's philosophy, the child is taught that no person is better than any other, and that there are no objectively right and wrong answers for him to grasp, since everyone's opinion is equally valid. The child is taught that individual grades are anachronistic, that competition is bad and group-effort is good, that assignments should be done collectively and that truth is determined "democratically" by majority vote. Each student is taught to value the crowd over the self, conformity over independence, emotional solidarity over rational judgment.

And when they become adults and their religious authorities, for instance, assure them that "Creationism" is just as scientific as the theory of evolution—or when their politicians warn them that industrial activity must be throttled because it will destroy mankind through global warming—or when the world's opinion-leaders tell them that self-sacrifice is noble and self-interest is evil—they apply the lessons they were taught in school. They do not independently judge whether facts and logic support such assertions; they simply defer to the group consensus.

As Dewey wrote, in explaining why the schools should focus on "socialization" rather than on cognitive skills: "The mere absorbing of facts and truths is so exclusively individual an affair that it tends very naturally to pass into selfishness. There is no obvious social motive for the acquirement of mere learning, there is no clear social gain."[31]

On one aspect, Dewey is correct. The "absorbing of facts"— which entails the *thinking* required to understand and make use of those facts—is indeed selfish. It is an act performed by, and only by, the individual. And his survival depends upon it. It depends upon the exercise of the mind—upon the learning of facts, upon the integration of those facts into wider and wider principles, upon the application of those principles to the task of living. All of this can be done only within the confines of each individual's brain. There is no collective thinking, any more than there is collective eating or collective breathing.

Your life and *your* goals demand *your* thinking—which is the core reason that the notion of a public interest that supersedes private interests is impossible. It is not society that enables the individual to exist; it is the individual who makes possible his own existence and, as a consequence, the existence of a society. Knowledge, discoveries, inventions, production, trade—*rational thought and action*—are all generated by the individual. Knowledge can be transmitted and shared—but it must first be *acquired*. How? By and in the mind of the individual. Goods can be traded—but they must first be *produced*.

How? By the choice and the effort of each individual involved in the transaction. Cause precedes effect. It is the individual, not society, who is primary.

There is no inherent conflict between the individual and society. The public does not ultimately benefit by sacrificing some of its members. The tenet of utilitarianism—"the greatest good for the greatest number"—is a cruel fraud, a recipe for genteel cannibalism. It is not in the interest of your two neighbors to seize your house and share it between them, even though they outnumber you. It is not in the interest of a racial majority to lynch members of the minority. Whether collectivism takes the form of sacrificing 49 percent of the population to 51 percent, or of sacrificing one man to the whole of society, there is no justification for it—neither morally nor practically. A civilized society is not ruled by the law of the jungle. It protects those who are in the minority, because it rejects the belief that "might makes right." And as Ayn Rand observed: "The smallest minority on earth is the individual. Those who deny individual rights cannot claim to be defenders of minorities."[32]

The premise of self-sacrifice is harmful to *all*. The good of society cannot be achieved through the cannibalization of any of its members. A society that adopts cannibalism is annihilating itself, not just its victim of the moment. It is establishing a *principle* of destruction, a principle by which today's eaters become tomorrow's eaten.

Just as there is no such entity as the public apart from the individuals who constitute it, so there is no public interest apart from the interests of each of those individuals. By espousing a policy of self-sacrifice, collectivism destroys the foundation on which all human life rests.

Is there any valid meaning, then, to the concept of a public interest? *No,* if it refers to something underived from, and opposed to, the individual's interest. But *yes,* if it refers to the actual interest of each individual who lives in a society.

The nature of the individual's interest is definable. It does not lie in leeching off others, but in self-reliance. It does not lie in sacrificing himself to others, nor in sacrificing others to himself, but in producing his own, rational values. It lies in dealing with others cooperatively and voluntarily, through mutually beneficial exchange.

With respect to political life in society, therefore, there is one basic value that is in the interest of all: freedom. Individual liberty is the common denominator of everyone's interests. Those interests are furthered, not when the government provides us with parks, or Mother's Day shrines or anthropological documentaries—but when it recognizes that each of us should be free to *choose* whether or not to create, or to utilize, such parks and shrines and documentaries. Unlike all the things typically held to be in the public interest, freedom is a value that does not arise from the sacrifice of some people to others. Freedom is in the interest of the public because, and only because, it is in the self-interest of each individual who makes up the public.

The doctrine of altruism, however, has a very different position on the value of freedom—as we shall see in the next chapter.

FIVE

ALTRUISM VS RIGHTS

IN THE WESTERN WORLD, WE VALUE THE IDEA OF FREE-dom. We understand that there should be restrictions on what others, particularly the government, may do to us. We recognize that each person has a realm—however it is defined—that must be safe from intrusion, a realm off-limits to others, a realm in which he is autonomous. We believe that the state should not have unrestricted power to do whatever it wants. We assume, in other words, that the individual has *rights*.

The altruist code is incompatible with this view.

Since it obliges you to subordinate yourself to others, altruism cannot regard you as an independent, autonomous being. Instead, your status is that of a servant—a servant to others, a servant to the collective. And a servant has no rights, only duties. A servant submits to the wishes of his master. Nothing of yours, therefore, is off-limits to the collective. There is nothing of yours to which you

---

may claim a *right*, since a superseding claim always belongs to those who *need* it.

To have a right is to be free to act on your own authority. It is to act by your own, sovereign judgment, without outside interference. Acting by right is the opposite of acting by permission. As John Locke, the originator of the principle of rights, states: "[E]very man has a property in his own person; this nobody has any right to but himself. The labor of his body and the work of his hands, we may say, are properly his."[1]

If you freely voice a political opinion, you are exercising your rights; if the law forbids unauthorized criticism of the government— if such thoughts are deemed contrary to the "public interest"—your rights are being denied. If you must obtain the approval of others before acting, you have no *right* to act, and are not free. Rather, you are living only by the sufferance of those others. Yet that is precisely the altruist-collectivist position: you exist only by the sufferance of society. That is, the individual enjoys no natural rights but only various privileges extended, or revoked, at the will of the collective.

If we must live for others, we simply are not entitled to be free. Auguste Comte, altruism's champion, declares that his philosophy

only recognizes duties, duties of all to all. . . . [I]t cannot tolerate the notion of *rights*, for such a notion rests on individualism. We are born under a load of obligations of every kind, obligations to our predecessors, to our successors, to our contemporaries. . . . Rights, then, in the case of man, are as absurd as they are immoral.[2]

The yoke of altruism permits you no independence. The ox secured to the plow, toiling for its master, does not get to decide whether or not to live as a beast of burden. In contrast to Locke's view that man has an innate right to his own life, the altruist's position is that man must sacrifice himself for the sake of society.

FREEDOM IS NEGATED BY A DUTY TO SACRIFICE

Many defenders of altruism, especially the conservatives, try to reconcile freedom and self-sacrifice. They argue that while you are morally obligated to sacrifice for others, you still have the full political and legal right to *choose,* without government coercion, whether and how to meet that obligation.

But this contention contradicts the underpinnings of altruism.

To recognize a right to choose would be to concede that the individual ought to decide how to conduct his life. It would be an acknowledgement that your life belongs fundamentally to *you.* But it doesn't, according to altruism—it belongs to others. And it is therefore up to them to decide how and when to collect what is due them. You have no right to shrug off your chains, any more than a debtor has a right to be free of his creditors. The collective has a claim on your existence. As Pope Paul VI expressed this view: "You are not making a gift of your possessions to the poor person. You are handing over to him what is his."[3]

If an employer chooses not to engage an obese person as an aerobics instructor, the altruist morality compels him by law to act against his choice and to sacrifice. If a medical provider, to avoid endangering himself, decides to treat an AIDS patient only within the protective facilities of a hospital, the altruist morality compels him by law to act against his decision and to sacrifice. The individual, "born under a load of obligations of every kind," is *not* free to choose how he lives. Only the collective is given that authority.

Religion provides an elucidating parallel. Those who take religion seriously believe that we all have a duty to serve God. They believe that we cannot arrogate to ourselves the decision of how to lead our lives. They believe that we must obey God, and that divine punishment awaits those who flout his commandments. (And when religion holds the reins of government, as in a theocracy, that punishment is meted out in this world, by the state.)

In its essentials, this is altruism's philosophy as well. It too declares that you exist to serve an entity above yourself, that the decision of how to conduct your life is to be controlled by that entity—and that if you don't voluntarily comply, you will be compelled to do so under threat of legal punishment.

The idea that man has rights contradicts the idea that man must be a servant. A servant, whether to God or to society, cannot be his own master. Only if his life is his own can he have the freedom to choose how to live it. (Obviously, this freedom includes the political right to choose to be an altruist and live for the sake of others. But it is only because an individual *is* the master of his own life that he can voluntarily decide to become a servant; someone who is a servant by nature, however, cannot choose to become anything else.)

And there is a deeper parallel to religion. Its claim that we must subordinate ourselves to God begins with a more fundamental claim: that the human mind is incapable of discovering the truth. Religion tells us to place our trust not in our intellect but in God, who will reveal the truth to us. Religion rests entirely on faith.

Faith is not synonymous with confidence, nor with conviction, nor with certitude—all of which are concomitants of reason. Rather, faith is the adoption of an idea in disregard of evidence. It is belief in defiance of knowledge. When the rational mind grasps that a sea cannot be parted with a wave of the hand or that the dead cannot be resurrected or that the earth is billions of years old, religion demands that such knowledge be jettisoned and replaced with faith—with faith in that which reason knows is not so. "Trust in the Lord with all your heart and lean not on your own understanding," the Bible exhorts.[4] Our minds are untrustworthy, the advocates of faith declare, and any conclusions based on the evidence of the senses and of logic are illusions. Surrender the intellect, they tell us, and believe in a supernatural being that is beyond our puny comprehension.

But since abandoning his rational faculty is abandoning his means of survival, the extent to which a person embraces faith is the extent to which he becomes dependent on someone else to keep him alive. Like a blind man clinging apprehensively to a sighted companion in the middle of traffic, the person who is not guided by his own mind must rely on some other consciousness to tell him how to navigate through all of reality. Religion instructs him to rely on the consciousness of God. It instructs him to give himself over to divine authority.

Faith spawns dependence—and dependence calls for servitude. If you have faith in God as your shepherd, you must follow, meekly as a lamb, whatever he tells you.

Altruism too anchors its doctrine in the groundwork of faith. As noted earlier, altruism has no answer to *why* you should sacrifice for others. It offers no rational justification for placing the lives of others above your own. Instead, it insists that morality is outside the province of reason. It requires you to accept its precepts on faith. The good, according to altruism, is determined by society, upon which you must be dependent for moral guidance. The good, it claims, is not what you rationally decide benefits you, but whatever others say benefits them. The good, it maintains, is for you to serve the collective faithfully. And to serve the collective is to submit to its dictates.

Only by upholding reason can one uphold *in*dependence, and thus freedom. To be guided by reason is to allow no intermediary between one's mind and reality. Because a thinking man forms his conclusions by his own judgment, he does not have to substitute someone else's consciousness for his own. He is not subservient to someone else's beliefs. He thinks for himself. He is confident in his ability to deal with reality. All he requires from people is to be allowed to follow his own mind—to choose his own goals, to produce his own values and to deal through trade with other, like-minded individuals.

The link between reason and freedom is evidenced throughout history. When societies are dominated by faith and mysticism, freedom suffers; when reason reigns, freedom thrives. For example, the West's medieval era was dominated by the church. No dissent from Christian doctrine was permitted. People lived as serfs, bound to their feudal lords, and everyone was bound ultimately to the edicts of the church. People lived in wretched poverty, which they accepted as their necessary fate because they were taught that this world is a sordid place and that man is an execrable creature. They were told that material values are base, that man is destined to suffer, that relief beckons from some supernatural dimension—but only for those who obey God's wishes in this life. From peasants to kings, everyone lived in dread of being punished for his sins in an afterlife. Since the church determined what constituted punishable sin, and since it wielded the threat of excommunicating transgressors and consigning them to eternal damnation in hell, it was able to keep people in thrall. They paid taxes to the church, bowed their heads to the clergy and dutifully complied with ecclesiastical directives. Their lives were rigidly circumscribed by church canon. The occasional heretics were tortured and burned at the stake. When various groups were deemed to be deviating from religious orthodoxy, the pope dispatched armies of crusaders to slaughter the heretics.

It was with the onset of the Renaissance that the rule of mysticism began to weaken. The Renaissance was a rebirth, a return to the culture that shaped Ancient Greece: the culture of reason.

People began to question received dogma. They began to think independently. Largely through the revival of Aristotelian thought, they again came to realize that man *can* understand the universe. They started to study, and to master, the natural world. This transformation evolved into the Enlightenment, as reason became widely established as man's guide to knowledge in science, in philosophy, in the arts, in politics—even, to a significant extent, in religion, with the spread of deism, whose premise was that even the Bible must be congruous with reason.

The political culmination of this centuries-long development was the creation of the only nation in history founded explicitly on the philosophy of individual rights: the United States of America. This country was the political product of the Age of Reason. As one of the Founding Fathers, Thomas Jefferson, wrote: "Fix reason firmly in her seat, and call to her tribunal every fact, every opinion. Question with boldness even the existence of a God; because, if there be one, he must more approve of the homage of reason, than that of blindfolded fear."[5]

America was founded on the conception of man as a rational, independent individual, not an unthinking vassal. America was born as a nation that would allow man to live in freedom, with the inalienable right to his own life, his own liberty and the pursuit of his own happiness, while government was limited to the task of protecting these rights. It was a nation which propounded the radical idea that the individual ought to be free to express any thoughts and to practice any religion, or none at all—along with the equally radical corollary that, to preserve such liberty, church and state must be separated.

A society that celebrates the individual has no place, and no need, for masters and servants. But if the individual must sacrifice himself—whether for the neighbors, for the proletariat or for the Fatherland—his rights disappear. If we want to uphold man's rights, therefore, we must approach the subject from the perspective, not of altruism, but of egoism.

THE MEANING OF RIGHTS

We now have to ask: what exactly do rights entail? Certainly, there cannot be a right to do whatever one wishes. What, then, does one actually have a right *to*—and why?

In order to live, a person must choose to think and to act—and must be left free to do so. For someone isolated on a desert island, the issue of freedom is meaningless: he obviously cannot demand that the trees and the rocks leave him alone. But when he lives among people, freedom becomes necessary, because what he needs to be free *from* is interference by others.

Rights secure that freedom.

Ayn Rand characterized a right as "a moral principle defining and sanctioning man's freedom of action in a social context."[6] The most fundamental, all-encompassing right is to that which engenders the very need for rights: man's life. Life requires self-generated, self-sustaining action. The right to life means the freedom to engage in such action. Your nature as a rational being requires you to gain the knowledge and the values that maintain and advance your existence. The right to life means that you should be free to take the actions you deem necessary for the furtherance of your life. It means that you should be free to follow your own judgment, in pursuit of your own goals. And, since life is impossible without the material results of one's actions, the right to life includes the right to property. Your property, like your life, is the product of your efforts. Without the right to acquire, use and dispose of property, no other rights could be implemented. The right to express ideas, for example, is pointless if nobody is permitted to own a pen, a computer, a lecture hall, a publishing house or a soapbox. Your only obligation toward others, then, is to acknowledge their possession of the same rights that you have, and to refrain from violating them.

By what means can rights be violated? *Only by physical force,* i.e., by physical action taken against someone without his consent. Physical force (which includes the *threat* of its use) disables the victim's tool of survival: his mind. It stops the individual from acting by his own choice. It compels him to act, not in accordance with his judgment of what is best for him, but in obedience to the commands of a gunman. Fraud also belongs in this category, since it is merely an indirect form of force: whether someone's money is taken by an armed robber or by the seller of a phony deed, his property is being expropriated. In either case, it is being taken without the owner's consent, and his rights are being contravened.

When people adopt the principle of rights, they disavow force and are able to live together peacefully and cooperatively. Man's rights, in other words, are a necessary condition for the existence of civilized society.

It is crucial to grasp the distinction between force and all other forms of human interaction. In response to something you've said or done, a person can raise a questioning eyebrow or wag a rebuking finger. He can ignore you, admonish you, ridicule you or write a tome condemning everything you've ever done. But none of these actions deprives you of your rights. You are still free to follow your own conclusions. Intellectual dissent directed against you does not compel you to do anything. A weapon pointed at your head, however, does.

Consequently, a free society categorically bars the use of force, whether initiated by an individual or by the state.

Of course, what is barred is *initiated* force. But force used in *retaliation*, against whoever initiates it, is morally obligatory. The corollary of the right to be left free is the right to repel all attempts to deny that freedom. The right to your life necessitates the right of self-defense. A criminal must be dealt with by retaliatory force, in order to preserve the rights of his (actual and potential) victims—a task that, in a civilized society, is delegated to government.

The rights you have are not primarily to an object, but to your *actions* (and, secondarily, their products). Your right to live is not the right to be *given* the means of living, but rather the right to achieve those means without obstruction by others. You have a right to work—which consists of the right to offer your services to any employer willing to hire you; you do not have a right to compel anyone to give you a job (or to support you if you cannot find one). You have a right to seek medical care—which means a right to be treated by any doctor who willingly accepts you as his patient; you do not have a right to compel anyone to treat you (or to pay your medical bills for you). You have a right of expression—which gives you the right to voice your opinions to those willing to listen; you do not have a right to compel anyone to provide you with a microphone, a website or an audience. The only objects to which you are entitled are those that are the consequences of your own actions—i.e., objects that you produce (or acquire voluntarily from others who have produced them) and that become your property.

Were you to have a *primary* right to an object—to food, to shelter, to a job, to health care, to a byline on an op-ed page—you would be forcing someone else to provide it, in abrogation of *his* rights. And there can be no right to violate rights. The rights you have when dealing with other people rest on the right of free trade. Since each person has a right to his actions and to the product of those actions, human interaction requires the consent of all parties. No one may be compelled to relinquish what is his on terms to which he does not agree. There can be no such thing as forcible "trade"—there is only forcible theft.

Rights are *individual* rights. It is the nature of the individual that generates the fact of rights. There are no collective rights. There are only the rights of each person to *his* life, *his* liberty, *his* property, the pursuit of *his* happiness. No association of people holds any rights that do not stem from the rights of each individual member of that group—rights that the individual has voluntarily assigned to the group. No transcendent rights are created through conglomeration.

Like "rights" to some object, "collective rights" are self-contradictory. Only individuals concretely exist and concretely act. To claim that the collective has rights, which supersede those of the individual, is to claim that some people are entitled to appropriate the efforts, and thus to infringe the rights, of other people.

Because rights inhere in the individual and because rights apply to the individual's actions, the rights of one man do not conflict with those of another. Everyone is entitled to the identical freedom: the freedom to act non-coercively. Within this context, everyone has the absolute right to live as he chooses. If you are unwilling to buy someone's car for the price he is asking, there is no clash of rights. Each party has the right to make or refuse a trade. No one's rights are violated by a failure to reach agreement, and each party keeps what is rightfully his. But if you steal his car, then only his rights are at issue, and you are breaching them. One man's rights end, in effect, where another's begin.

People may have legitimate disputes over how to interpret a clause in a particular contract or how to determine the precise location of a certain property line. These are questions of application. But there can be no disputing the fact that the basic *principle* of rights—the principle that allows disputes to be resolved in a peaceful manner by acknowledging each individual's sovereignty over his own life and property—is in the interest of all who want to live in a civilized society.

Rights are your guardians against anyone who would subject you to force. And the greatest potential threat they protect you from is the government. They declare that, as long as you refrain from using force, you may live your life without interference from the state.

Many people believe that property rights are something grudgingly doled out to us by the collective. A major philanthropic foundation, espousing this position, stated: "We need to change the policy of allowing property owners to think they can do what they want with their land merely because it's theirs. Owners must come to realize that whatever rights they have in land they happen to own are rights accorded them by society."[7] Others take this premise further and contend that *all* rights are merely creations of the state, consisting of whatever the government decides its citizens should be granted. So if our politicians happen to allow us to speak our minds, a right to free speech materializes; if they establish a national orchestra or provide meals to schoolchildren, then we acquire a right to free art or to free lunches. In this view, the "right" to receive a welfare check becomes as valid as the right not to be murdered.

In this viewpoint we again see the influence of Hegel's collectivism, in particular his belief that the state is the ultimate, and unconstrained, moral authority. It is a viewpoint, as explained by two modern-day professors, which holds that rights are nothing more than "powers granted by the political community," that anything "qualifies as a right when an effective legal system treats it as such by using collective resources to defend it" and that therefore all "apparently non-welfare rights [e.g., the right not to be robbed, raped or killed] are welfare rights too."[8]

But if the government does not base its actions on the principle of individual rights, what standard does it use? If a right is whatever our politicians wish it to be, how do they determine what laws should and should not be enacted? Only arbitrarily. A government not guided by objective principles is an unchecked government—and anything goes. Such a government dispenses ersatz rights and violates genuine ones at whim, as it subjectively decides what does and does not represent the mystical public will.

It is the principle of rights that ought to shape and constrain all decisions made by government. A proper government is a *limited* government, and the inalienability of rights is what sets the limits.

"Individual rights are the means of subordinating society to moral law," Ayn Rand said. They are "the extension of morality into the social system—as a limitation on the power of the state, as man's protection against the brute force of the collective, as the subordination of *might* to *right*."[9]

Man by nature has rights; the role of government is not to confer them, but to *defend* them. This responsibility to protect our rights consists of two parts—and altruism opposes both. The first part is to disavow the use of initiated force. And as we've seen, altruism enthusiastically endorses such use: it demands that the government forcibly take from the "haves" and give to the "have-nots." The second part is to wield force in retaliation against those who have initiated its use. Here too altruism objects. Give the criminal another chance—the altruist urges—show compassion rather than condemnation, rehabilitate him rather than incarcerate him, try carrots rather than sticks, blame society rather than the individual. Whenever a person does something to warrant punishment, the code of self-sacrifice demands that his victim turn the other cheek. Need—according to altruism—preempts rights.

THE SOLE POLITICAL SYSTEM THAT REPUDIATES SERVITUDE

The various social systems devised by man throughout history subordinate the individual to the collective—to the tribe, to the community, to the nation. They have typically subjected the citizen to massive applications of force, from the confiscation of wealth to wholesale slaughter. But there is one exception. There is one social system that rejects the tradition of servitude and consistently upholds the rights of the individual: capitalism.

Capitalism rests on the premise that your life belongs to you alone, and so therefore does your property. It regards the individual's rights as absolute, and no appeal to the collective good is allowed to override them. As long as force or fraud is not being used, no restraints are placed on an individual's actions, from the opinions he may express to the profits he may earn.

Under capitalism, the answer to the question: "What is the proper function of government?" is provided by the answer to a more fundamental question: "What facts give rise to the very need for a government?" Although force must be used against anyone who initiates it, we cannot have every person acting as his own judge, jury and executioner. Anarchy creates only a vast new threat to our rights. If everyone is allowed to use force at his own discretion, the innocent would never know when they might be a target. People would live under constant danger of being attacked by anybody who felt that someone had wronged him. Society would consist of armed camps, with everyone's rights in perpetual jeopardy. So while retaliatory force is the means of protecting rights, its employment must be placed under *objective* control. We need an entity exclusively empowered to use force, under rules that are publicly known and that are objectively derived, defined and applied—that is, rules molded by the principle of individual rights. This entity is government. In order to avoid threatening the rights of his neighbors, and to protect his own rights, the individual must delegate his right of self-defense to the government.

To carry out this function, a proper government creates mechanisms for dealing with violations of its citizens' rights. Once the legislature passes appropriate laws prohibiting the various uses of force, and identifying government's response to lawbreakers, institutions must be put in place to implement the laws. Three institutions are necessary: the police, to protect us from domestic criminals; the judiciary, to interpret and apply the law by adjudicating (civil and criminal) disputes; and the military, to shield us from threats of force from abroad.

This is essentially all that a government ought to do. When force has been initiated, government must step in decisively to stop it; when no force has been used, government has no role to play.

Capitalism is the system required by a republic, as established by America's Founding Fathers. In contrast to a democracy, in which nothing is exempt from the rule of the majority of the moment, a republic places stringent limits on the powers of the state. In a republic, the state may *not* simply do whatever the majority wishes. It is restrained by the idea of individual rights, with a constitution defining explicitly what the state may and may not do. If a majority democratically voted to execute someone for expressing unpopular views—as happened to Socrates in ancient Athens, for example—its decision would not be valid. If a majority democratically voted simply to ignore the Constitution and to install a dictator—as the Reichstag did, for example, in granting Hitler limitless power in Nazi Germany—its decision would not be valid. America was founded on the premise, not of a transient "will of the people," but of enduring, inalienable rights. Inalienable—even in the face of a numerical majority.

Since government is an agent of the citizenry, it is proper that we vote for our political representatives. But in a republic, our representatives have authority only within a severely circumscribed sphere, a sphere defined by the principle of individual rights. The majority does not decide whether rights should be recognized; it decides only on the specific *form* in which rights are best protected. Congress may legislatively determine, say, which actions constitute a breach of contract or an infringement of a book's copyright. But it cannot vote to nullify all contractual agreements, and it cannot vote to eradicate an author's rights and allow the government to appropriate his work. Government exists to protect our rights; it cannot vote them away.

In a fundamental sense, government does not produce any values. It is an instrument of force. When acting properly, it prevents criminals, domestic and foreign, from destroying the values that private individuals have created. But when it goes beyond its proper boundaries, government itself becomes the destroyer.

We need government to exercise retaliatory force because that task cannot be done privately without endangering the individual's rights. But everything else—everything outside the realm of force—can and should be done privately. There is no place for government in education, medicine, agriculture, energy, housing—or any area of life in which people deal with one another voluntarily. When government injects itself into such realms, it goes from protecting rights to violating them. When it decrees how much doctors may charge or what crops farmers may grow on their land or whether cars must contain airbags, it abrogates the rights of people who are willing to deal with one another on terms other than those being dictated by the state.

Outside the province of retaliatory force, there are no "essential services" that government must provide. Anything for which there is an authentic demand by the public—i.e., anything for which individuals are willing to spend their, not others', money—will be supplied by the free market. Under capitalism, everything from libraries and post offices to hospitals and subways will be privately produced and privately owned. But when there is no market demand, we will not be compelled to pay for government-mandated "public goods."

I should stress that when I use the term "capitalism," I do *not* refer to the hybrid, half-free, half-controlled economy that has long been operating in America. I use the term to mean full, laissez-faire capitalism, with the same separation between economy and state as should exist between church and state.

Genuine capitalism will not allow the government to place any roadblocks in your path. You will not need to pay for government licenses before you can open a shoe-shine stand. You will not have to spend hundreds of thousands of dollars for a government-mandated taxi medallion that gives you permission to use your car to pick up riders on the street. You will not have your application to medical school rejected because the government wants preferential treatment given to certain groups.

Nor, on the other hand, will the government be able to dole out any favors under capitalism. If you want to provide a cable-TV service, you will not be granted an exclusive, competition-barring franchise. If you want to raise cattle or cultivate orchards, you will not be able to lobby Washington for tariffs on imported beef or fruit. If you want to build a football stadium, you will have no access to financing through state-issued bonds. Companies will not receive government subsidies, loans, grants, debt-guarantees or bailouts, no matter how stridently they invoke the "public interest." Everyone will be on his own. The government will not be allowed to use its coercive powers to push any-one down or to help anyone up.[10] (With respect to acts of charity, the same two rights-preserving rules apply as to acts of trade: no one will be compelled to engage in them, and no one will be prevented from engaging in them. Charity, too, will be your decision, not the state's.)

Man lives by production, an act of the mind—and capitalism is the system that allows the rational, unfettered mind to function. The process that transforms untouched parts of nature into goods ready for human use—the process that converts barren dirt into fertile farmland, or pools of buried hydrocarbons into gasoline and heating oil—is an intellectual one. It is directed by the intelligence of people who are left free to think and to reap the benefits of their thinking. Whether people choose to be entrepreneurs or poets, capitalism allows them to progress as far as their abilities take them.

THE "EQUALITY" FRAUD

Since altruism holds as its standard the needs of the collective rather than the rights of the individual, it regards capitalism as evil. It re-viles the selfishness inherent in private property and private profit. Socialism is its ideal, with all resources controlled by and for the sake of "society as a whole." The altruist accuses capitalism of creating inequality by establishing a rigid class system in which some people are privileged while others are not. Socialism, the altruist contends, erases distinctions among people and treats everyone the same. So-cialism, he says, achieves true equality.

This is a key argument by capitalism's opponents—and a specious one. Just as the altruist smears selfishness by linking it to the actions of a predator, so he smears capitalism by linking it to the kind of inequalities that arise under despotic governments. The altruist points to societies in which, for example, noblemen were given license to seize the belongings of peasants, or in which Hindu "untouchables" were executed for marrying outside their caste. The same type of inequalities, he claims, typify capitalism. But if equality is to have a valid meaning, it is *capitalism* that makes everyone equal. It is capitalism that achieves what is meant when the Declaration of Independence states that "all men are created equal"—namely, an equality of *rights.*

In non-capitalist systems, rights are dismissed. There, political inequality reigns, as the laws favor some and disfavor others. There, some are allowed to loot and kill, as others are allowed to be looted and killed. But under capitalism, where the law is based on the universal principle of individual rights, this is impossible. Capitalism permits no legally privileged elite. Just as rights apply to all, the law applies to all. No one can wield force with impunity, because the rights of every individual—rich or poor, famous or obscure—merit full protection. The state may not ignore violations of your right to control your property or your right to choose whom to marry. Politically and legally, capitalism renders all citizens equal.*

---

* I do not use the term "libertarianism" to describe this system because—like the term "liberalism" in the nineteenth century—it has, sadly, been expropriated by those who use it to stand for a system incompatible with individual rights.

An equality of rights, however, is not what altruists seek. Their actual goal is an equality of *condition*—particularly, the condition of material wealth. Why, the altruist demands, should one person have a bigger house or a bigger bank account than another? Why shouldn't we all enjoy equal riches?

The very question arises only from a collectivist premise. It assumes that everything, and everyone, belongs to society. It assumes that any wealth you enjoy is an expropriation from the collective. It assumes that we are all interchangeable cells of the social organism and so no cell should receive a bigger paycheck than any other.

But we are not cells. Each of us is a sovereign, volitional individual. Wealth does not ooze, causelessly and anonymously, out of a social corpus. It is *created*—it is created by the efforts of the individual, and he therefore has a right to it, irrespective of how much or how little his neighbor has. If man has a right to live his own life and to pursue his own values, then the goal of society must be to ensure, not equal incomes, but full liberty to all—including the liberty to earn as much money as one can, and to keep it safe from all prospective confiscators. Morally, the fact that your neighbor has something you lack does not entitle you to it. Economically, your neighbor's assets do not create debits in your account—i.e., you are not worse off just because he is better off. And legally, your

---

There is now a tacit anarchism in libertarianism, under which the state is equally condemned for using force where it shouldn't, as in economic matters, and where it should, as in the military defense of the nation. For elaboration, see my book *Libertarianism: The Perversion of Liberty.*

neighbor's unwillingness to share his possessions with you is not an act of force.

Capitalism engenders intense hostility because of its one central characteristic: justice. Capitalism is the system that embraces justice. The greater your ability and productiveness, as judged by the choices of all who participate in the free market, the greater your rewards. If the salary of a corporate CEO is one hundred times higher than that of a janitor, it is because the CEO produces that much more wealth. The janitor may have more needs, but the CEO *deserves* far more compensation for his role in the company's functioning.

One man's production does not come at the price of another man's non-production. The CEO does not get rich by making the janitor poor. To the contrary, the janitor benefits from what the CEO generates (far more than the CEO benefits from the activities of the janitor). The wealth created by the CEO makes it easier, not harder, for the janitor to increase his. Whenever anyone produces goods in a free market, others gain. When the CEO makes possible the construction of new houses or the discovery of new medicines, more goods (and better jobs) are now available to enhance people's lives, including the janitor's. And if the janitor cannot afford that new house or new medicine, then he forgoes it. Nothing is being taken from him. His life is not diminished, and his rights are not threatened, merely because he lacks enough money to buy something that wouldn't exist in the first place without the CEO and the company he runs.

There is no virtue to equality as such. Treating all people justly, for example, entails treating the honest person very differently than the dishonest one, or the criminal very differently than his innocent victim. There certainly is a virtue in *consistency* when applying a proper standard—and under a consistent application of the individual-rights standard, everyone is entitled to keep whatever he has earned. Which means that some people will make much more money than others. It is not inequalities in wealth, but rather the attempts to *eliminate* them by forcible redistribution, that constitute an infringement of rights.

Capitalism rests on egoism. But a large number of people want to uphold capitalism—or, rather, some mongrelized version of it—without abandoning their altruist ethics. Afraid to offer a moral defense of self-interest, they try to validate capitalism on ostensibly practical grounds. In pursuing self-interest, they say, one is led by an "invisible hand" to promote what is good for all. A man opens a shoe store in order to make money for himself, and—lo and behold!—his customers are better off by virtue of their new shoes, and his employees are better off by virtue of their new jobs. The general standard of living rises, and the profit motive turns out to be good for the general public. The nominal defenders of capitalism are quick to make clear that they do not morally condone selfishness. But within the framework of a free market, they claim, selfishness is transubstantiated into altruism.

This justification for capitalism has become widely accepted. All businesses invoke it. Whenever they are criticized for caring too much about profits, they do not assert their right to work for their own benefit. Instead, they defensively point to the benefits they shower upon others. When New York City landlords, for instance, campaigned to loosen rent-control regulations, they did not argue that they have a right to their property and are entitled to set their rents at whatever level people are willing to pay; rather, they argued that decontrolling rents would help the poor and hurt the rich.[11] When Walmart, for instance, was accused of keeping its wages too low, its response was to boast about its employee health-care program and its considerable contributions to charity.[12]

From Adam Smith to supply-side economists, the proponents of capitalism take the ethics of altruism as an uncontested given. They cower in the face of accusations of selfishness. Yes, they concede, capitalism does promote selfishness, but only as a necessary evil. They see capitalism as a wealth-producing machine whose output advances society's well-being. If socialism were somehow able to churn out the goods, they argue, we would have a perfect system. Since socialism cannot do so, they reluctantly tolerate capitalism as the most efficient means of attaining altruistic ends.

But this is a perversion. The capitalist system could not function if its practitioners actually achieved altruistic ends. Consider the shoe-store owner, who sells his products at a profitable price. Along comes the altruist to speak up for the people who can't afford the price, but who need shoes nonetheless—cut the price in half for them, he insists. Then there are the homeless, he notes, who can't afford to pay anything, but who desperately need shoes—they should get them for free. Then there is the job applicant who has never managed to hold a position for more than three months, but who really needs a paycheck—fire one of your competent workers and hire him, the altruist says. Then there is the manufacturer whose products are shoddy and whose service is unreliable, but who is burdened with an ill mother and an expensive gambling habit, and urgently needs your business—start buying your supplies from him. Etc. Etc. If it accepted the goals of altruism, could any company, or capitalism itself, remain in existence for long?

Altruism represents the antipode of production. Economic production is the *creation* of wealth—a process of generating goods, which are exchanged for other goods, with every participant injecting his own productiveness into a continuous cycle of ever-increasing prosperity. Altruism, however, aborts this process because it is the *sacrifice* of wealth. It is the renunciation of riches—it is the destruction of values—it is the surrender of the producer's work to the non-producer's needs.

But isn't a profit-making business in fact good for its customers and its workers? *Not by altruism's standards.* The customers get only what they pay for, and the workers are remunerated based only on what they are worth to the employer. What is repeatedly taking place is a trade—and altruism despises trades, since they give people nothing other than what they deserve. Only trafficking in the unearned—only dispensing and receiving sacrifices—constitutes the good, according to altruism.

Observe how altruists evaluate our history.

The explosion of wealth under capitalism lifted the masses out of the wrenching privation of the pre-industrial age. In Western

Europe, it took from 1 A.D. to 1500 A.D. for total wealth to quadruple; that same quadrupling was achieved during just the last forty-five years of the twentieth century.[13] In the Western world today, the average person takes for granted riches that were inconceivable even to the very wealthiest before the advent of capitalism. Capitalism has spawned countless life-transforming innovations, from electricity to automobiles, from vaccinations to organ transplants, from jet travel to smartphones. It has enhanced the lives of billions of people, many of whom would never even have existed without the burst of productiveness let loose by capitalism. Life expectancy in Western Europe was about thirty-six years in the early nineteenth century; it is now more than double that.[14] Around the turn of the nineteenth century, as the Industrial Revolution was taking hold, the world was able to sustain a population of less than one billion; today the figure is over seven billion. In fact, the number by which the population managed to inch upward during the 3,000 years prior to the Industrial Revolution was equaled in just over 100 years once it began.[15]

Despite all this, capitalism is disparaged by our so-called humanitarians as crudely immoral. Why? Because these results were not generated self-sacrificially. The benefits of capitalism have been achieved, not by the Mother Teresas among us, but by the Thomas Edisons, the Henry Fords, the Andrew Carnegies, the Cornelius Vanderbilts, the Sam Waltons, the Steve Jobses—i.e., by independent-minded, profit-seeking individuals. The idea that any genuine benefit can accrue from such selfish efforts is abhorrent to altruists.

They do not view burgeoning private wealth as something good, but as an *evil*. Every dollar you save, every object you purchase, is a dollar or an object that someone in need is not getting. The richer you become through capitalism, the greater is the unfulfilled need of those who lack what you have, and the greater is your "theft" from them.

Capitalism frees us all to engage in selfish, life-promoting activities. Even those who hold the most unskilled, menial jobs gain enormously from a free market, which creates the productive machinery that allows the undemanding motion of pushing a button or a lever to become remunerative work.

Capitalism benefits even the relatively few who are totally disabled and who must rely on charity for their survival. Capitalism not only fosters the development of the medical technology and the drugs that such people require to remain alive and functioning, it also makes possible the widespread affluence that enables individuals to be generous toward those who, through no fault of their own, cannot support themselves.

But capitalism does *not* benefit everyone. Those who believe they are entitled to *demand* assistance—those who believe others have a moral duty to provide for them—will find capitalism unaccommodating. Those who seek the unjust will not be aided by a system built on justice.

To the question, then, of whether capitalism is practical, the answer is yes, by the standard of egoism; but no, by the standard of altruism. Whether something is deemed practical depends on what the deemer wishes ultimately to practice. And if the goal is to reward need rather than merit, then any element of capitalism becomes *im*practical.

Altruism's objectives simply cannot be achieved through the system of capitalism. An end cannot be contradicted by its means. The altruist's aim is not for you to benefit others—which you accomplish through every self-interested trade you make—but for you to *sacrifice* for others. And since capitalism disavows selflessness, it cannot become the means of attaining it.

A system built on the foundation of rights is incompatible with a system built on the foundation of need. To the extent that capitalism is implemented, therefore, altruism is negated; to the extent that altruism is implemented, capitalism is negated.

Anyone's profit-making activity under capitalism enriches others—but that fact is merely a consequence, not a moral justification. Such benefits are not the *standard* by which the activity should be judged. Nor are they the actual motivation of producers. When businesses claim to be driven by the selfless desire to help others, they deceive no one. All they accomplish by such feeble, appeasing dissimulations is to confirm their enemies' tawdry view of self-interest, while displaying their own guilt and hypocrisy.

There is only one logical way to defend freedom and capitalism—and it is ably demonstrated by Hank Rearden, one of the heroes in the novel *Atlas Shrugged*. An industrialist, Rearden has devoted ten years of relentless, painstaking effort to the development of a revolutionary metal that could earn him a fortune. But Washington wants to dictate the terms under which he will be allowed to profit from his product. To serve the "public interest," he has been ordered to sell his metal only at government-established prices, only in government-specified quantities and only to government-approved customers. He is now on trial for refusing to comply. His accuser, trying to elicit from him a statement of remorse, admonishes him in court: "You wouldn't want to give support to the widespread impression that you are a man devoid of social conscience, who feels no concern for the welfare of his fellows and works for nothing but his own profit." To this, Rearden defiantly replies:

> I work for nothing but my own profit—which I make by selling a product they need to men who are willing and able to buy it. I do not produce it for their benefit at the expense of mine, and they do not buy it for my benefit at the expense of theirs; I do not sacrifice my interests to them nor do they sacrifice theirs to me; we deal as equals by mutual consent to mutual advantage—and I am proud of every penny that I have earned in this manner. . . . I could say to you that I have done more good for my fellow men than you can ever hope to accomplish—but I will not say it, because I do not seek the good of others as a sanction for my right to exist, nor do I recognize the good of others as a justification for their seizure of my property or their destruction of my life.[16]

Like all moral principles, rights require an uncompromising defense—a defense that unapologetically identifies rights as a *selfish* value. Living free rather than as a slave is a value to *you*. To possess rights is to be an end in yourself, not a duty-bound means to the ends of others. They are *your* rights, and others may not violate them, no matter how much they brandish their needs.

The unambiguous choice we face, therefore, is this: either selfishness and freedom—or altruism and slavery.

SIX

THE COLLECTIVIST STRAITJACKET

IN DEFINING THE CENTRAL PURPOSE OF GOVERNMENT—as we've seen in defining a system of ethics—there are two antithetical approaches, deriving from one's fundamental view of man. The individualist approach, which regards man as a rational, productive being, asks: "What political system will allow him to take the actions necessary to sustain his life?" The collectivist approach, which regards man as an ineffectual, perpetually needy entity, asks: "What political system will allow him to be taken care of by society?" The first approach results in a system of self-interest and individual freedom, as envisioned by America's Founding Fathers; the second leads to a system of self-sacrifice and collective control, as exemplified by the modern welfare (or "entitlement") state.

The welfare state is the system now adopted by America, and most of the Western world. In it, government is seen as indispensable in providing its citizenry with the means of coping with the demands of living. According to the tenets of altruism, people are morally entitled to have their unfulfilled needs met; the welfare state ensures that they are *politically* entitled as well. Food, housing, education, medical care—if people lack it, the government supplies it.

In 1944, Franklin Roosevelt proposed the radical idea of a "Second Bill of Rights," under which everyone would be guaranteed by law "a useful and remunerative job . . . adequate food and clothing and recreation . . . a decent home . . . adequate medical care . . . protection from the economic fears of old age, sickness, accident and unemployment . . . [and] a good education."[1] Today, that proposal is hardly controversial. "There are certain economic rights . . . to the basic necessities of life"—the American Civil Liberties Union asserts—under which, for instance, "a homeless person has a right based in the Constitution to have shelter."[2]

This view, of course, is simply a secular version of the Biblical injunction to sacrifice for the needy. "As followers of Jesus Christ and participants in a powerful economy," the National Conference of Catholic Bishops explains, "Catholics in the United States are called to work for greater economic justice." How? By implementing the principle that "people have a right . . . to secure the basic necessities of life, such as food, clothing, shelter, education, health care, safe environment and economic security."[3]

So the government distributes the food, the clothing, the shelter, the health care—but only by first expropriating the funds from the *producers* of wealth. The premise behind "economic rights" is that some people have the right to demand that the government compel others to sacrifice for them.

TO BE TAKEN CARE OF IS TO BE CONTROLLED

But if people have to be taken care of by the state, if they cannot be left on their own, then they cannot be trusted to make decisions by themselves. If they are to be fed, they must be told what food is to be permitted them. This is why, for example, we are given state-approved nutritional requirements by the Department of Agriculture, in the form of "food pyramids" and "food plates," which must be followed by all schools participating in the National School Lunch Program. This is why the government tells food packagers to reduce the salt content in their products—it is why restaurants in various localities are prohibited from serving dishes containing trans-fats—it is why the mayor of New York City demanded a ban on the sale of large cups of sugared soda.

Our politicians rule with a paternalistic mentality. It is under this mentality that edicts are issued against gambling, against smoking cigarettes, against riding motorcycles without helmets and against buying liquor on Sundays. It is under this mentality that a social services agency locks up a 400-pound man in a mental institution's eating-disorder unit, because his extreme obesity is not "in the interests of that person's health or safety."[4] It is under this mentality that the Bowery Mission, a soup kitchen in New York City, is forced to throw away donations of fried chicken for the hungry—because the food was cooked with trans-fats.[5]

The premise of paternalism is the premise of control.

The welfare state seeks to shape the lives not just of the poor, but of everyone. The altruist philosophy regards man as essentially helpless. Since we are deemed incapable of meeting our needs without the sacrifices of others, we must be not only ministered to, but directed by, the collective. Do we, for example, need to put aside money for our retirement? The government gives us Social Security, but prohibits us from opting out and relying entirely on a private system of savings. Do we have a need for mail delivery? The government provides it, but bars us from having regular letters delivered by carriers other than the Postal Service. Do we need schools? The government establishes a public education system, but refuses to allow parents the choice of taking the money being spent on public schools and using it instead to send their children to private schools.

We must be managed by the state, the collectivists insist. Just as the unsupervised child, they argue, will always choose a dinner of ice cream and cookies over one of fish and broccoli, the unsupervised adult too will follow his desires of the moment. We cannot be trusted to do what is best for us, since we are unable to exercise rational thinking. As a *New York Times* editorial contends, adamantly opposing the idea of giving parents a choice of schools: "What of parents who are unable or unwilling to choose? . . . Some parents will always lack information or initiative."[6] And what about those who *do* act to acquire information and *do* show initiative? They are dismissed as mere exceptions—and, according to altruism, the exceptional must always be sacrificed to the non-exceptional. Those who choose to think must be sacrificed to those who choose not to.

Every government intervention into what can be done privately and voluntarily is an act of paternalism. In the same way that we are made to buckle the seat belts in our cars and install carbon-monoxide detectors in our homes whether we want to or not, we are made to finance public schools, public libraries, public transportation and public theaters whether we would willingly pay for such services or not.

A welfare state is a regulatory state. It spawns a vast network of bureaucracies designed to restrict our actions "for our own good." While prosecuting fraud is a vital function of government, this is not what the regulatory apparatus does. Let me repeat that: *regulatory agencies are not essentially concerned with fraudulent behavior.* When they regulate cigarettes, it is not because people today are unaware of the health dangers of smoking. When they prohibit private gambling, it is not because people are duped into believing that it is a risk-free activity.

Or consider the transaction bizarrely called "predatory lending"—i.e., the issuing of loans that the government declares are too difficult for the borrower to repay. The government objects to such loans, even when no one is being misled about the terms and no one is being forced to accept them. The payday loan, a short-term, high-interest (and high-risk) loan collateralized by the borrower's next paycheck, falls into this category. It is outlawed by several states simply because the financing terms are said to be too onerous. By whose standards, though? Certainly not by those of either the lender or the borrower, each of whom judges that he is better off if the loan is made than if it isn't. According to the paternalistic mentality, however, we are unable to know our own interests.

The regulators share the contemptuous view of human nature expressed by a man who took out a number of payday loans, could not repay them—and then condemned the lender for having made the money available to him: "It's sort of like a twisted person that's standing on the street corner offering a child candy. He's not grabbing the child and throwing him into a van, but he's offering something the child needs at that moment."[7] The regulators believe that the borrowers unthinkingly grab the money, and that the lenders unthinkingly offer it, with neither party stopping to ponder whether the loan can actually be repaid. So the parental state steps in, chides everyone for acting foolishly and takes away the candy.

What government regulations prohibit is not fraud, which is covered by numerous legitimate laws, but the free judgment of adults. The regulator's premise is not that the irrational is possible to man, but that it is *inescapable*—that a non-functioning intellect is our normal condition—that, like beasts or infants, we cannot be reasoned with and must therefore be compelled to do whatever our overseers decide.

A long line of philosophers lies behind this notion of man's intellectual impotence. From Plato, with his transcendent "World of Forms," accessible only through some special, mystical insight; to Hume, with his mind-shrinking skepticism; to Kant, with his assertion that our very possession of consciousness distorts the world "as it really is"; to Hegel, with his "dialectical logic" and glorification of contradictions; to today's postmodernists, with their claims that our convictions are merely the product of unavoidable, subjective prejudices—there is one dominant message: the individual's mind is inadequate to the task of knowing what is true.

So we must have a nanny-state to guide us. We must abstain from foods that are salty or sugary. Restaurants must post the caloric content of its foods, whether customers demand such information or not. We may not patronize florists, manicurists or lemonade-stand operators unless they are duly licensed by the government. The state must take us tightly by the hand and lead us. Only our nanny knows what is best for us.

This view permeates all aspects of today's culture. We now have, for example, a popular school of thought called behavioral economics—"a radical critique of the standard assumption that human beings behaved in economically rational ways," a *New York Times* columnist wrote. "The behavioralists, as they are known, pointed out that this assumption was ridiculous." Consequently, they insist that the government must forcibly stop us from acting stupidly. For instance, this columnist noted, since some people fail to refill their prescriptions and then become seriously ill, the behavioralist would have the government require "an annual fee for a drug, rather than the current system of charging people separately for each prescription refill, which gives them a reason not to get the refill."[8]

The book *Nudge*, a best-seller co-authored by two proponents of behavioral economics, became quite influential in Washington. It argues that since people do not know what is good for them, the government must "nudge" them in the desired direction. For example, people often fall asleep under sunlamps and get burned. The solution, the authors say, is to compel manufacturers to install automatic cut-off switches. Couldn't people simply be allowed to *choose* whether to buy a lamp with a cut-off switch? No, because people cannot be relied on to make intelligent decisions:

> [There is] a distinction between two kinds of thinking, one that is intuitive and automatic, and another that is reflective and rational. . . . The activities of the Automatic System are associated with the oldest parts of the brains, the parts we share with lizards. . . . Humans sometimes go with the answer the lizard inside is giving, without pausing to think.[9]

The TV character Homer Simpson is trotted out by the authors to illustrate this point:

> In a commentary on gun control, Homer once replied to a gun store clerk who informed him of a mandatory five-day waiting period before buying a weapon, "Five days? But I'm mad now!" . . .

One of our major goals in this book is to see how the world might be made easier, or safer, for the Homers among us (and the Homer lurking somewhere in each of us).[10]

Thus, because our "inner Homers" prevent us from thinking rationally, we need government guardians. We need to be protected, not from those who would defraud us, but from *ourselves,* from our own deficient brains.

This view is not promulgated out of honest conviction. Those who insist on depicting man as a helpless, deterministic creature have to evade the patent evidence to the contrary. After all, with every action a person takes, he can introspectively grasp that he *does* have a choice. He may blind himself to the consequences of his decisions, but he still knows that he is free to remove those blinders by choosing to think. He may mentally drift, passively following whatever random emotions he happens to experience, but he knows that he can choose instead to activate his mind. That is, he realizes that at any waking moment he can decide to exercise his capacity to reason. The fact of human volition—the fact that man's consciousness, unlike a lizard's, does *not* work deterministically and that whenever someone does act like Homer Simpson he does so by choice, not by irresistible, mechanistic forces—is introspectively self-evident.

And if one shifts from introspection to extrospection, from focusing on the inner mind to focusing on the external world, he can see the historical progress of man, from a primitive caveman to the modern explorer of distant planets and of subatomic particles. He sees the products of human reason—the science, the technology, the industry, the continual expansion of knowledge, the unprecedented improvements in our standard of living. He sees that what was once a barren wilderness is now paved highways and glowing skyscrapers and humming factories. He sees the efficaciousness of man's rational faculty. He sees that regardless of how often people may act unthinkingly, their ability to think remains intact. He sees that to define man as a rational being is not to deny the capacity for irrationality; it is to assert that we are always *capable* of using reason—and that our lives depend on it.

Those who keep pushing the claim that man is inherently non-rational—while the regulators somehow aren't—simply want a justification for ruling others (as well as an excuse for their own irrational behavior). The ardent paternalist is a seeker of power. He desperately wants to portray man as requiring a leash—and wants to be the one holding it.

REGULATIONS VICTIMIZE BOTH
PRODUCERS AND CONSUMERS

People generally understand the effects of abrogating intellectual freedom. They understand that when the government censors a newspaper, for example, it is not just the publisher, but every reader, whose rights are violated and whose interests are harmed. When it comes to economic regulation, however, many believe that only business is impaired, while consumers are helped.

But there, too, *everyone* is being victimized.

A free market is the manifestation of people's uncoerced choices. In any transaction between consenting adults, the choice each makes is whether to accept the other's terms. If a gasoline station sells its product at a given price, requires you to pump the gasoline yourself and accepts no credit cards, you choose whether or not to make the exchange. The seller does not force you to agree; he simply offers you something that *wouldn't exist if not for his efforts*. Since reality requires that the goods on which human life depends be *produced*, the fact that you must pay the producer is not coercion, but voluntary trade. You are always free to open your own gasoline station—or to drill your own oil well. But you are not free to demand that someone else create the goods for which you then unilaterally decree the conditions of sale.

A trade occurs only when each party determines that his life is improved by it. If you decide that the terms of sale are unacceptable, you are not injured. You are then in the exact position you would have been in had the seller never existed. You are not worse off by forgoing what someone else has created and was never yours.

When government intervenes, however, you *are* worse off. Since the intervention occurs only when people are otherwise willing to make an exchange, every restriction on a seller is simultaneously a restriction on a buyer. When self-service gasoline stations or "predatory" mortgages are forbidden, the freedom of both producer and consumer is being abridged. Both are being prevented from obtaining what each judges would further his interests.

What about respecting the choice and the interests of the person who *wants* the government to intervene—the motorist who wants to have an attendant pump his gas when the station owner would not voluntarily provide one, or the tenant who wants his rent regulated so that he pays only half the amount the landlord could get from another willing renter? The very question is self-contradictory. One is entitled to a choice only over one's *own* person and property. There can be no right to freely choose that which renders free choice and rights impossible: the initiation of force. When a person cries that it is unfair to deny him some product merely because he is unwilling to accept the owner's terms—well, that's the attitude of every thief, who wishes to rectify the fact that people won't voluntarily give him something for nothing. It's an attitude that is not tolerated in a free market—but is readily accommodated in a regulated economy.

In a free market both parties gain; under government regulation, however, one man's loss is the price of another's gain—a gain that is fleetingly short-term. In the long run, the regulatory state does not help even its intended beneficiaries. Just as common thievery is not a practical way of living, neither is thievery committed by law. No one ultimately benefits in a society that dispenses with rights. No one ultimately benefits from institutionalized parasitism.

What about issues of safety? Even if government should stay out of economics, doesn't the importance of human health necessitate government oversight?

Quite the contrary. *Because* this sphere is so vital, it is even more imperative that the coercive power of the state be kept out.

The choice to live—the choice to pursue our values—entails risks. Since we are not immortal and not omniscient, we must face the possibility of failure, of loss, of injury, of death. Risk is unavoidable in life; only death is risk-free. Inherent in the process of living and of goal-achievement is the process of deciding what risks are worth taking. From a decision to play tennis to a decision to undergo heart surgery, we each choose the level of acceptable risk in any given situation. A rational person takes the appropriate precautions to minimize risk and enhance the opportunity for success. But every individual decides, based on his knowledge and his values, what risks are tolerable for what benefits. Even when specialized knowledge is required, the affected individual still ultimately decides. Whether a doctor gives you a medical diagnosis or an auto mechanic assesses the status of your car's brakes, you decide whom to consult and whose advice to follow. In the same way that you judge whether a given product is worth the price, you judge whether a given activity is worth the risk. By making such judgments, you are acting to attain your values and to advance your life.

Government intervention does the opposite.

When the regulator steps in to "protect" you, he is harming you. Every time you ride a bicycle or climb a ladder, you've decided that the benefits justify the risks. But when the government restricts the types of bicycles or ladders you may use—or forbids them outright— you are prevented from achieving your ends. Every act by the safety regulators forbids you from taking a risk that you have concluded *is* worth taking. The state substitutes its judgment for yours. You are forced to give up what you have determined is best for you.

Observe, for instance, the effects of our pre-eminent federal safety agency, the Food and Drug Administration.

When the FDA declares that some drug is hazardous to your health, it does not seek your agreement. It imposes its decision on you, whether you concur or not, and keeps you from using the drug. (I'll focus here on drugs, rather than food, though in principle there is no difference.)

If the FDA's role is to reassure people that a drug is safe, so that they are willing to use it when they otherwise wouldn't—if the agency believes that people will take medicine only if it is approved by the government, rather than by some private entity—why is coercion necessary? Why doesn't the FDA announce its evaluation and then grant people the freedom to accept or reject it?

The FDA, like any regulatory body, has only one basic function: to say no—or rather, to say no and to force us to abide by that pronouncement. The sole act the FDA can perform that an unregulated market cannot is to stop us from using medications we believe are beneficial. The FDA exists, not to keep us from being deceived by drug manufacturers, but to keep us from judging for ourselves what is good for us.

The drug Lotronex, for example, treated the painful, life-disrupting affliction of irritable bowel syndrome. Ten months after the medication had been approved, and used by some 300,000 people, the FDA pressured the manufacturer to withdraw it from the market because of newly discovered side effects. Inflammation of the colon had developed among seventy users, and three deaths were possibly tied to the drug. According to a *New York Times* report, "patients and their doctors say there is no other drug for them to switch to, no other effective treatment for their condition. While the illness is not fatal, many patients say the sudden attacks of diarrhea ruin their lives, and they want to take their chances with the drug."

The story of one such patient was presented in the article:

Mr. [Corey] Miller, a 30-year-old architect in Atlanta, knew that Lotronex had caused serious side effects in some patients and had been linked to several deaths. But he had suffered no ill effects. On the contrary, Lotronex was the only drug that had ever helped him, stopping the severe abdominal pain and diarrhea caused by an illness called irritable bowel syndrome.

"It was a miracle medicine for me," he said.[11]

Nonetheless, the drug was removed. Hundreds of thousands of Corey Millers were thereby consigned to unrelieved misery—a misery compounded by the agonizing knowledge that a cure existed but was unavailable to them because the government would not allow them to choose whether the benefits outweighed the risks. The FDA's condescending, paternalistic outlook was perfectly conveyed by an organization, Public Citizen, which had petitioned the FDA to withdraw the drug. As described in the *Times* story: "The group insisted that irritable bowel syndrome was not a serious enough disease to warrant the risks posed by Lotronex. . . . [Public Citizen argued] that it made no sense to use a drug with potentially life-threatening side effects for a disease like irritable bowel syndrome, which is debilitating but does not kill people."[12]

Corey Miller, and numerous others like him, obviously disagreed. When he learned that Lotronex was being withdrawn from the market, the *Times* reported, Miller, "who had been taking it for about eight months, began stockpiling it. He persuaded a doctor to write an extra prescription, and went to twenty drugstores in search of the recalled pills." He and his doctor wanted to be the ones deciding whether to dismiss his condition as "not a serious enough disease to warrant the risks." That is, he and his doctor wanted to be the ones deciding whether the harm from *not* taking the medicine was greater than the harm from taking it. But the FDA would not permit that.[13]

The FDA was not concerned about people being defrauded. It did not demand the retraction of any false claims about Lotronex. It did not issue factual information about the drug and allow people to decide for themselves. It simply disapproved of the decisions people made, and prevented them from taking a drug they wanted.

By what right does the government do this? Your life is not collective property. It should be *your* right to decide what values to pursue, including what risks to take in pursuing them. Even if we ascribe to the regulators the best of motives, even if we stipulate that they are the most honest, most conscientious people to be found, why should they be empowered to make the decisions for all of us? Why can't private citizens be allowed to disagree with the regulators about the suitability of a drug for a particular condition? (Even among the FDA's own doctors and scientists there is often disagreement on whether to approve a drug.) Why shouldn't everyone be free to rely on his own physician and make the decision for himself? Why should there be any role here for government?

THE SELFISH MOTIVE TO MAKE SAFE PRODUCTS

But—it may still be asked—don't the *producers* need to be regulated? In the absence of an FDA, what would protect us from adulterated medicines sold by profit-seeking manufacturers?

It is precisely the goal of profit-seeking, however, that is the public's best assurance of safe and effective products. A company maximizes its income not by foisting snake oil on unsuspecting customers and then disappearing overnight, but by offering them genuine value. It wants customers to be satisfied with their purchases so that it can continue, and expand, its business.

Any enterprise that plans to remain in operation relies on an indispensable asset: a positive reputation. The greater a user's concern about the quality of a product, the more vital to the user—and the more profitable to the producer—is the fact of the producer's reputation. Which hamburger, for example, would you feel safer eating: one from a long-established, Michelin-rated restaurant, or one from some transient street peddler? Would you consider the meat from the two sources equally safe simply because each displayed the same government-issued food permit?

A free market rewards companies whose products perform as advertised, and punishes those whose products don't. To earn a marketable reputation, a business must safeguard the integrity of its products. It must pay unceasing attention to the quality of its output, since just one lapse can undo years of developing a good name. Businesses that thrive under capitalism are those that take a long-range outlook. They realize that short-term corner-cutting leads to long-term ruin.

When a company allows shoddy products to be sold, the problem isn't that it is too greedy—but that it is not greedy enough. The problem is that it lacks the commitment to making as much money as it can by avidly guarding its reputation.

Only a bureaucratic mentality, one that is sealed off from the real world of supply and demand, could fail to grasp that a profit-seeking firm, unlike the government, cannot afford dissatisfied customers. Only a bureaucratic mentality could be unaware of why people receive incomparably more efficient and attentive service at, say, FedEx than at a post office. Or at Hertz than at the Department of Motor Vehicles. Or at any entity whose customers exist by choice than at one whose customers exist by force of law.

Only a bureaucratic mentality could believe that the pursuit of profit makes a company oblivious to the safety of its airplanes, its buildings, its construction cranes, its food, its drugs. It is precisely in such areas that conscientious attention to quality is *most* profitable. Again, the more urgent the customer's concern about a product's safety, the more he is drawn to the companies with the best reputations.

Businesses that are free to compete will continually work to enhance the value of their products, including the value of safety. They will compete to offer ever-higher levels of safety at ever-lower prices—not out of selfless concern for the welfare of others, but out of a selfish desire to produce what their customers want. In the pharmaceutical field, each company will develop what it regards as the best methods of research, of clinical testing, of manufacturing, of packaging—all of which will be judged as good or bad, not by a regulatory bureaucracy, but by the people who voluntarily use, sell or endorse the company's products. These people include a long chain of interested parties—doctors, hospitals, pharmacies, medical journals—all of which, of course, have their own reputations to preserve.

Thus, for assurances of safety we need not rely solely on the assumption that a company will act in its long-term interests. In a free market, third parties arise to provide us with needed information. We now have private certifiers, such as Underwriter Laboratories, Good Housekeeping, Better Business Bureau, *Consumer Reports* and VeriSign, giving their seal of approval to various products and companies, in areas ranging from electrical appliances to automobiles to Internet security. Similarly, in the absence of regulations, private entities would assess particular drugs (as they actually did in the United States prior to the FDA's preemption of that task). They would present facts and evaluations, which your doctor could utilize in deciding whether to prescribe any medication. These certifiers too would compete with one another; they too would have to depend on their reputations. But unlike a government agency, all such private firms would have to function by *persuading* people that their data, and their conclusions, were reliable.

Fundamentally, the producer's interests align with the consumer's. A company's success rests on its ability to supply what people choose to buy. If there is a market for, say, Lotronex, it means that doctors willingly recommend it to their patients. It means that people are given the level of safety they *choose*—i.e., the patients whose doctors judge that the medicine is too risky for them will not take it; those whose doctors judge it to be worth the risk, will.

The fact that a drug has undesirable side effects does not make it unsafe—any more than a bathtub is unsafe simply because you can drown in it. If your physician informs you that 2 percent of aspirin-takers suffer gastrointestinal hemorrhaging, but you nonetheless accept his advice to take aspirin, you are deciding that the benefits outweigh the risks. You are not being deceived, as long as the manufacturer does not lie about the product's properties.

If and when an act of fraud does occur, the offending company should certainly be prosecuted. If a manufacturer falsely claims that its aspirin can never cause hemorrhaging, or if a batch of aspirin turns out to be only sugar pills, people are being cheated and the government should step in to protect their rights. Laws against the deceptive sale of goods are perfectly legitimate—but the mere fact that deception is not impossible is no basis for regulatory controls.

Under proper laws, government takes action whenever there is real evidence that an act of fraud is being, or will be, perpetrated.

But in the absence of evidence, there should be no presumption that a business is guilty until it can prove its innocence. The fact that under certain circumstances some wrongdoing is imaginable does not constitute evidence. The fact that sugar pills can be made to look like aspirin does not warrant an assumption that every aspirin-maker is guilty. The fact that a particular manufacturer was guilty of selling a counterfeit product is not grounds for requiring *every* manufacturer to prove in advance, to some bureaucrat's satisfaction, that its product is not a fake. There is no justification for *preventive law,* which is the essence of government regulation—any more than the possibility of drunk driving justifies banning all alcohol, or the possibility of sending anthrax through the mail justifies the government's interception of all letters.

Obviously, the profit motive does not guarantee that any particular product is safe. *But no such guarantee is ever possible.* Since people have free will, a company's executives may evade their long-term interests and try for the "quick buck." They may well choose to be dishonest. But so, of course, can government agents—*and with far greater impunity.*

If a private company is known to engage in fraudulent practices, it quickly loses customers. But when FDA officials are found to have been crooked, they may be fired but the agency's operations continue unabated.

Imagine that we had a genuinely free market. Compare, then, a well-regarded private certifying company with today's FDA. Which one's inspectors could more easily extort a bribe in exchange for a favorable evaluation? Which one's inspectors could more easily withhold approval simply because the company under examination was not sufficiently obsequious? Is it the private certifier, which knows that its clients are always free to take their business elsewhere, and which is strongly motivated to prevent any tarnishing of its reputation? Or is it the FDA, which holds a monopoly grip over a company—a life-or-death power to approve or reject its products—and which can impose the most arbitrary demands upon that company?

Consider, alternatively, a fly-by-night outfit that wants to receive a positive assessment for some dubious drug it is trying to market. Or perhaps it wants a negative assessment assigned to a competitor's product. Which inspector could be more readily bought off—one from a private agency, whose revenues depend on the trust it earns from its voluntary customers, or one from a government agency, which enjoys an unrestricted source of funding from coerced taxpayers? Just as the profit motive gives private businesses a greater incentive to act efficiently, it gives them a greater incentive to act honestly.

And there is a further, more fundamental distinction. A private firm's goal is production. The regulator's goal, however, is to *impede* production. The job of a regulator is to stop people from willingly engaging in actions they judge to be in their interest. His orders are to adopt the role of an all-knowing parent who prevents his children from making undesirable choices. The regulator knows that he must above all avoid permitting something that he might later be told he should have prohibited.

The FDA, for example, receives no praise for approving a drug. Its annual award to the employee who best exhibits "excellence and courage in protecting public health" is intended for those who block or retard the marketing of a drug, not for those who allow it. As former FDA commissioner Alexander Schmidt observed: "I am unable to find a single instance where a Congressional committee investigated the failure of the FDA to approve a new drug. But the times when hearings have been held to criticize our approval of a new drug have been so frequent that we aren't able to count them."[14]

Studies have shown that the mere delay in approving drugs that are being safely used in other countries causes thousands of needless deaths every year[15]—to say nothing of all the useful drugs that get developed but never approved, or all the ones that are never developed in the first place because of regulatory burdens. But by the nature of the FDA's mission, its focus is not on the pain endured and the lives lost as a result of its saying no; its dominant concern is to escape being blamed for saying yes.*

---

* Let me briefly note that the thalidomide tragedy—which is invariably raised when deregulation is discussed—is categorically *not* evidence of a need for an FDA. Thalidomide, taken by pregnant women to treat morning sickness, was found in 1961 to cause severe birth defects. But at the time, the effects of drugs passing through the placenta were not well known—not to the scientific community and *certainly not to the FDA*. The FDA's own requirements did not include testing for fetal malformations. There was typically no testing on pregnant subjects, neither animals nor humans. (See Vasilios Frankos, "FDA Perspectives on the Use of Teratology Data for Human Risk Assessment," *Fundamental and Applied Toxicology*, vol. 5, 1985, p. 615.)

The maker of thalidomide had complied with all the FDA's guidelines. Approval of the drug in the United States was delayed because the FDA's investigator was concerned about reports of peripheral neuritis in long-term users of thalidomide—*not* about the drug's effects on fetuses. A company has every

It is the *regulators* who injure us. It is the regulators who cause us to suffer unnecessarily, by insisting that we give up the means of alleviating our illnesses and of enhancing the quality of our lives. By preventing us from weighing risks and benefits—by shielding us from the supposed harm of using some product, while subjecting us to the harm of *not* using it—they make our lives worse. They compel us to take what we regard as the more damaging course of action. They forcibly override our judgment, because they believe we are incapable of knowing what is really good for us.

SELF-INTEREST MAKES OBJECTIVE THINKING POSSIBLE

The obvious question at this point is how the regulators themselves can know what is good. If people are impulse-driven dupes, who

---

incentive to prevent the kind of disaster caused by thalidomide. What it doesn't have is omniscience. Undiscovered medical knowledge, not greedy indifference toward the possibility of deformed babies, was at the root of the problem.

One can act only on what one knows, and the acquisition of medical knowledge can be a demanding, arduous task. It is a complex process to judge the data about a particular drug. One must ascertain the disorders it can treat, its possible side effects, its interactions with other drugs, the relevance of other conditions a patient might have, etc. The full properties of a drug are sometimes not known, and not *knowable*, until after a vast number of people, over a long period of time, have used it. Even the most extensive testing on animals may not be sufficient. This is part of the inherent risk one accepts if one wants the benefits of a new drug.

In fact, with respect to thalidomide, it seems that even if fetal testing *had* been conducted on pregnant animals, the danger to humans would probably not have been discovered, since subsequent research showed that thalidomide has no effect on the fetuses of most animal species. (Conversely, a drug such as aspirin deforms the fetuses of most animal species, but not those of humans. Aspirin would have been one more of the beneficial drugs made unavailable by the FDA had today's regulations been in force at the time of its introduction.)

cannot be trusted to overcome their "inner Homers," what makes government officials supposedly immune? What makes *them* the adults while the rest of us are regarded as helpless children?

There is only one answer: their altruistic motives.

Self-interest is disparagingly regarded as a corrupting force, not just morally, but *cognitively*. In this view, the person who benefits from some action is incapable of thinking objectively about it. Whether seeking to acquire a tan or to find a treatment for his cancer, he will not think logically. He will be unable to think about the effects of leaving a sunlamp on too long or of taking a dangerous drug. Instead, he will be consumed by his desires, unmindful of any potential harm to himself.

If self-interest distorts thought, who then *can* think logically about such matters? Only the *disinterested*. Only if one has nothing personally to gain, in this view, can one judge objectively. And who is this disinterested party? The collective—the state. Since a collectivist government does not act selfishly, it becomes the only entity deemed capable of making the decisions that affect your interests.

Thus, you are allowed to donate your kidney as an act of charity, but you are legally forbidden from selling it to someone who needs it. Why? Because your desire for the money supposedly makes you heedless of the risks. Approximately 100,000 people in the United States are on waiting lists for kidney transplants, but kidneys are available for fewer than 15 percent of them, with several thousand on that list dying annually.[16] Even though many more people would be willing to provide a kidney for transplant if they were paid, our federal nannies say no. They do not permit a donor the choice of financially benefiting from giving up a kidney, just as they do not permit a desperate patient the choice of paying for one. They declare that the ill are better off forever tethered to the misery of dialysis, or even dying, than being the recipient of a kidney tainted by commerce. We cannot be trusted to make a rational decision, they say, when we have a selfish interest in the outcome.

Take another example. There is much opposition to immigration. One major reason is the fear that immigrants will mooch off the American taxpayer by collecting welfare, enrolling their children in public schools, receiving Medicaid, etc. Why not allay this legitimate concern by allowing people to come into this country, but barring them from all government aid? Why not allow entry only to those who are committed to being productive, self-supporting individuals? Let each prospective immigrant choose whether he wants to come into this country under such conditions. Let each one choose whether his interests are better served by living in America and forgoing government assistance, or by remaining in his own country. Let both citizen and immigrant profit, at no one's expense. But no, this arrangement would be intolerable to our public leaders. They regard it as unfair to immigrants. They maintain that government overseers are necessary to prevent the immigrant from making an impetuous decision he may come to regret. So they are willing to refuse entry to most of the people longing to come to America—they are willing to consign them to the wretched poverty and despotism of their native lands—in the name of protecting them from themselves.

The same disgraceful premise is behind all regulatory interventions. The collectivists believe that a private company is always eager to make an extra nickel today, even at the cost of bankruptcy tomorrow. They believe that without the disinterested stewardship of a Federal Aviation Administration, our planes would be unsafe; without a Housing Department, our elevators would be unsafe; without a Transportation Department, our cars would be unsafe; without an Agriculture Department, our farm products would be unsafe. They believe that both the makers and the users of such products, since they are motivated by self-interest, are in thrall to their immediate urges and are unconcerned about issues of safety. They believe that only our paternalistic guardians, by selflessly focusing on the "public interest," are able to engage in objective, practical thinking.

And the same premise is behind a peculiar double standard. The crash of a commercial airliner or the explosion of an oil rig is taken as proof of corporate indifference to safety, eliciting calls for tighter government control or even outright nationalization. But the collapse of a municipal dam or bridge, or the uninhabitable squalor of many government-run housing projects, is taken as proof, not of government ineptitude and a need for privatization, but of the plight of a dedicated though sadly underfunded agency that requires a bigger budget.

Similarly, bankers were widely accused of causing the financial crisis of 2008 by recklessly issuing sub-prime mortgages to people unable to repay them. But the government officials whose policies made such recklessness possible were never held accountable. The ones who championed Fannie Mae and Freddie Mac, the quasi-governmental bodies created precisely to underwrite the kinds of mortgages that would not meet a free market's standards—the ones who applauded the Federal Reserve's goal of an expanding money supply and artificially low interest rates, which made mortgages unrealistically appealing to borrowers—the ones who urged the lowering of lending criteria in order to meet the Department of Housing and Urban Development's edict to make an increase in home ownership a national priority—the ones who compelled the banks to expand their loans in poorer neighborhoods as a sign of "non-discriminatory" lending—the ones who encouraged imprudent corporate behavior through a policy of bailing out companies that were "too big to fail"—*these* were the people who not only escaped culpability, but were often the very ones placed in charge of revamping the financial system to prevent a repeat of the disaster.

When Enron was found to have cooked its books, or when Bernard Madoff was caught running a Ponzi scheme to cheat his investors, such duplicity was widely regarded as intrinsic to capitalism, and new, sweeping regulations were imposed on all publicly traded companies and on all hedge funds. But when the federal government engages in far more devastating fraud, no one is outraged. The Social Security program, for instance, is administered in a manner that would cause the head of any private annuity to face criminal charges. Instead of setting aside a retirement fund for workers, the program spends every dollar, in arch-Ponzi fashion, the moment it is collected. It incurs an unfunded liability of over $20 trillion, which can never be paid out of currently projected tax revenues and which represents a debt burden of close to $200,000 on every U.S. household.[17] The wealth wiped out by the program *every two weeks* exceeds all the money lost through the scams of Madoff.[18] And the typical worker receives far smaller returns from Social Security than if his "contributions" were privately invested rather than publicly spent.[19] Yet there is no huge outcry. To the contrary, the paternalists' indignation is provoked only by any suggestion that the individual should be allowed to determine how and whether to save his own earnings.

Underlying all elements of the regulatory state is the belief that decisions we make based on self-interest are irresponsible and self-destructive, while decisions made *for* us, by our disinterested guardians, ultimately benefit us. It's the belief that unless we are controlled we become predatory producers and brainless consumers. It's the belief that selfishness dooms us to failure because it transforms us into creatures of emotion, rendering us blind to the future consequences of our actions.

But the paternalists have it exactly backward. If left free, the individual *can* achieve enduring success. It is the standard of self-interest that *demands* logical, long-range thinking—and the public-interest standard that makes it impossible.

Yes, when self-interest is involved—when one's values are at stake—emotions are generated. But they do not distort our mental functioning, unless we allow them to. The occurrence of emotions is indeed automatic; what we do about them, however, is not. We need not act on what we feel if it contradicts what we *know*.

Emotions play a vital role in life, but not a cognitive one. They are subconscious responses based on our past thinking (or non-thinking), but they do not *replace* thinking. When we experience an emotion, we are not identifying a fact of reality. Our feelings cannot tell us whether we can afford to buy a new car or whether we should vote for nationalized health care. It is *reason* that is our means of knowledge. It is only reason that can tell us what is true. And knowing the truth—and acting on it—is the essence of self-interest.

If you have a life-threatening disease, would you not be motivated to find the best doctor, the best medicine, the best hospital available to you? Would your self-interest not induce you to go through a process of *thought* to determine what course you ought to pursue? Would you not undergo an examination even if the procedure *felt* uncomfortable? Would you not seek out the results of a crucial medical test even if you *felt* fearful about what it might reveal? Would you not be guided by the *facts*—by the facts pertaining to your long-range interests?

Undoubtedly, some people in such circumstances would try to evade the truth. They might blank out the diagnosis they received, they might rationalize away the implications of their illness, they might eschew medical treatment in favor of prayer and faith-healing, they might wallow in an alcoholic haze. But then it is not self-interest that incapacitates them; it is their unwillingness to acknowledge what self-interest demands: a commitment to reality.

If we truly want to be selfish, we will—contrary to the claims of altruism—*think*. We will objectively focus on the facts. We will be cognizant of the consequences of our actions, rather than drift into mindless emotionalism. We will rationally choose our goals and the means of achieving them.

The irrational does reign, however, when these decisions are made for us by a disinterested, paternalistic state. As I've noted, there are no rational principles for wielding force in the name of an indefinable public interest. There are no objective guidelines for disposing of the income and the lives of other people. There is only short-term political expediency.

If, for instance, you are planning for your retirement by contemplating a private annuity, you can logically determine what is best for you. You can assess the relevant facts about yourself (e.g., your financial assets, your health, your anticipated expenses) and about the annuity (e.g., the price, the promised returns, the viability of the issuing company, the existence of competing products), and then decide whether buying it is in your interest. But when the architects of the Social Security system do the planning for you—when it is not their money at risk but yours; when the costs and the benefits are based not solely on financial and actuarial data but on political considerations; when government secures "customers" by holding a gun to the head of a worker today while promising him a payout backed by a gun held to the heads of the workers of tomorrow—the result is a ramshackle, short-range program designed by our politicians' "inner Homers" and doomed to bankruptcy. It is the selfless paternalist, not the individual pursuing his self-interest, who acts non-objectively and destructively.

The central error of the paternalist is the belief that he can benefit us by forcing us to act in a certain way. But the good cannot be attained by force. For adult human beings, the good requires *chosen* values. Just as one cannot be physically coerced into recognizing what is true, one cannot be physically coerced into recognizing what is good. Nothing can be of value to someone who chooses to disvalue it. Threatening someone with violence to get him to practice the violin does not make the instrument a value to him. Incarcerating an ascetic in a penthouse suite at the Ritz-Carlton does not cause him to value material luxuries. Even the value of staying alive cannot be forced on someone. If a person with a debilitating, terminal disease decides he wants to commit suicide, he does not benefit from being coerced into living. He may be bound by physical restraints, he may be medicated against his will, he may be fed intravenously—but he is not receiving any *value*. An individual's good cannot be achieved through bypassing his volitional faculty.

To the contrary, the victims of force—regardless of what motivates the ones who initiate it—are always harmed. To live, man must be free to observe, to understand, to judge, to evaluate, to decide—to *reason*. Force negates reason. The mind does not function by the jerk of a nanny's leash or at the point of a regulator's gun. When you are prevented from using your mind to choose your values and your actions, your basic tool of survival is disabled.

Economic controls, like intellectual controls, are tools of oppression. Forbidding the unlicensed sale of lemonade or the unauthorized delivery of a letter or the unapproved marketing of medicine is no different from forbidding the unsanctioned publication of a newspaper. As Ayn Rand noted: "*Intellectual* freedom cannot exist without *political* freedom; political freedom cannot exist without *economic* freedom; *a free mind and a free market are corollaries.*"[20]

SACRIFICING THE RATIONAL
TO THE IRRATIONAL

I've said that paternalism is the product of a collectivist philosophy. Yet on the surface it seems that the paternalistic regulator is concerned about the welfare of the *individual.* The regulator wants him to wear his seat belt rather than be injured, to avoid fatty foods rather than risk disease, to take safe medicines rather than suffer harm from dangerous ones. Isn't that the opposite of the demand that the individual surrender his well-being for the sake of the collective? Doesn't the nanny-state want each citizen to selfishly improve his life?

No.

In a welfare-regulatory state, the individual is insignificant. He is only a means to society's ends. The individual is told, in effect: "Society serves your needs by providing your schooling, your medical care, your subways and buses, your mail delivery, your pension. You must be able to carry out the tasks by which you in turn serve society. You are a cog in this vast social machinery and you must be maintained in good working order." The reason the individual is an object of concern is the political equivalent of the reason a farmer is concerned about the health of his pigs and chickens: they provide him with his bacon and eggs.

The premise that the individual cannot know what is good for him ultimately translates into the premise that the good of the individual does not matter—more precisely: that the good of the individual is an illusory notion—more precisely still: that the good of the individual *is defined by* the needs of the collective. Let's look again at the FDA to see how this idea manifests itself.

When evaluating a drug, the FDA does not use the same standard you or your doctor would in deciding whether you should take it. For instance, clinical data showed that Iressa, a drug for lung cancer, shrank tumors among certain people, such as those who had never smoked. Nonetheless, several years after approving it, the FDA banned its use for all new patients because, as noted in a news story, the drug "did not prolong lives in the lung cancer population *as a whole.*"[21] (Emphasis added.)

This is the metaphysics of collectivism: the assumption that we exist not as individual human beings, but as one all-encompassing organism with interchangeable components. In this view, it does not matter that a medication may be good for one person but not for another. To the collectivist, the unit of value is the "population as a whole," and a single, comprehensive ruling must be made for all—a ruling reached by having the government disinterestedly weigh the gain to a few inconsequential parts against the (supposed) harm to the whole. Accordingly, even if you are among those who are helped by a drug—even if you are dying and the drug is your only hope—you will not be permitted to take any medicine deemed detrimental to the "population as a whole."

When studies showed that the cancer drug Avastin was delaying the progression of tumors by an average of almost three months, an FDA advisory committee decided that the benefit was not worth the risk of side effects and voted to withdraw the drug as a treatment for breast cancer. Any individuals who *were* being helped by Avastin were deemed irrelevant. In response, some people mounted a protest. As reported in the press: "[A]bout a dozen women, many of whom said the drug was saving their lives, and some cancer support-group advocates pleaded with the FDA and the advisory committee to keep the drug available."[22] One of the tragic victims, a woman whose cancer was being successfully treated by Avastin, said plaintively: "A panel of six . . . decided that we are statistically insignificant. How do I explain that to my 4-year-old and 7-year-old?"[23]

There is only one explanation, and it was publicly offered by a member of that advisory committee: "The agency has to look at protecting a larger number of patients. Sometimes they have to make a decision that doesn't favor individual patients, but it's on the basis of the whole."[24] That is, the decision is made by the standard of the "collective good."

But how is this carried out in practice? An individual is able to judge whether some medicine is good for *him*. He can weigh the costs and the benefits, based on facts germane to his life. These facts pertain both to his particular medical condition (e.g., his responsiveness to alternative treatments) and to his particular values (e.g., whether some side effect, such as occasional dizziness, is a mild inconvenience or an intolerable impediment to his chosen profession). The individual can determine whether a small possibility of slowing his cancer outweighs the risk of taking a drug that has been only partially tested. A *collective* calculation, however, is impossible. There is no collective entity whose condition, values and interests can be measured. There is no way to ascertain whether or not a drug offers a "net benefit" to society. Does the use of aspirin, for instance, result in some total number of cured headaches and averted strokes that offsets some other total number of gastrointestinal hemorrhages and anaphylactic reactions? How many extra months of life for how many cancer patients on chemotherapy counterbalance how many additional cases of drug-induced illnesses or deaths? There is no rational answer to such questions. Since only individuals concretely exist, the FDA's policy of deciding "on the basis of the whole" can mean only what collectivism always means: some individuals must be sacrificed for the sake of other individuals. Accordingly, even the terminally ill will not be allowed to try a drug that has been rejected as "too risky."

And exactly who is being sacrificed to whom? To understand that, let's look at another drug vetoed by the FDA: flibanserin. By acting on the central nervous system, it offered a new treatment for women suffering from low sexual desire. However, while clinical trials showed that patients did experience some increased sexual satisfaction, the effects were "not robust enough to justify the risks," according to the head of an FDA advisory panel.[25]

This was not just a case of the FDA's refusing to allow prospective users and their doctors to judge for themselves whether the benefits outbalanced the risks. There was a deeper issue here, as articulated by a professor of psychiatry who opposed the drug. Testifying before the panel, she said: "Is there a small group of women who could benefit from medical intervention—probably." Nonetheless, the professor argued, if flibanserin gained approval, "the much larger group of women without any medical reason for their sexual distress will inevitably be misinformed and misled into thinking that there is a pill that can get them the sex life they read about, the one they think everyone else is having."[26]

Keep in mind, again, that the regulator's concern is not about fraud. There are plenty of laws under which to prosecute a manufacturer for making false claims about its product. No, the concern expressed above applies when no misrepresentation is taking place. The regulators want to ban an effective drug because some people may misuse it. They want to keep people from being misled—not by false advertising, but by their own fantasies about the drug's properties. But since it is always possible for some people to believe that a drug will do something it can't, consider the full implication of this concern.

If the FDA were worried that people lacked accurate information about a drug, it would simply publicize its own findings and allow patients and their doctors to make an informed judgment about whether to use the medicine. But the doctrine of altruism does not permit this. After all, if people are merely provided with medical information, the demands of the needy are not being fully met. The

FDA can describe what a particular drug is and is not supposed to do, it can present the consequences of misuse, it can explain the need to consult a physician—but what if people fail to listen? What if they ignore the evidence because their "inner Homers" have taken over? What if they obstinately wish to believe that some pill will magically cure their ailments or "get them the sex life they . . . think everyone else is having"? As long as people are allowed any freedom in making their own choices, there will always be some unmet needs—i.e., the needs of those who do not wish to make rational choices.

You may have a severe illness, for which you want to take an unapproved drug. You may have taken steps to inform yourself about the prospects for success and about possible side effects. You may have discussed the situation at length with your doctor. You may have studiously assessed the pros and cons, and then decided to use the drug. You are making a thoughtful decision—but you will be stopped, for the sake of the people who might make a thoughtless one. You must be sacrificed, you are told, so that the state can take care of the needs of the non-thinkers.

This argument can be made, of course, not just about medications but about *everything*—which is precisely what the collectivist does. Any product, from mousetraps to mutual funds, can be improperly used, particularly by those who do not care to acquire the requisite knowledge. Nothing, therefore, is exempt from the tentacles of the regulatory state. To protect the needy, the government must control everyone's actions.

It does not matter that an unapproved drug might be your only chance for survival. You must be prohibited from taking it—not because the prohibition will help *you*, which it obviously won't, but "on the basis of the whole." This is how the paternalist attends to your welfare: he makes sure you fulfill your duty to the collective. Fundamentally, he seeks to prevent you, not from making the wrong choice for *your* well-being, but from choosing your well-being as your standard—or, rather, he seeks to prevent you from misunderstanding what your true well-being consists of. His goal is to make sure you do what is *really* good for you—and the good, as defined by altruism, is the self-sacrificial.

Collectivism maintains that the individual must sacrifice for society—and society, as seen by the collectivist, *is* the needy. And who is more needy than the people who willfully refuse to take responsibility for their own lives, under the belief that society ought to shield them from their own irrationality? Thus the government regulates the medicine you may use, because other people might be tempted to take it when they shouldn't; it regulates your retirement program, because of those who might squander their savings; it regulates your educational choices, because of those who might make foolish decisions about the schools to which they send their children; and it regulates your intake of food, because of those who might be oblivious to their health requirements. You are forbidden to choose—because of those who do not wish to be burdened by the onus of choice. You must sacrifice your freedom—because of those who are indifferent to freedom. Everyone must be dragged down to the level of the worst, and be shackled to their needs. This is how the individual becomes subservient to society.

In the altruist's mission to sacrifice the "haves," the target is not simply the rich. It is, more broadly, the knowledgeable, the diligent and the responsible—who must subordinate themselves to the ignorant, the indolent and the irresponsible. Altruism demands that we provide for the needy, and the neediest of all are those who will not undertake the effort, the *thinking*, that human life requires.

It is for their sake that we must allow ourselves to become wards of an oppressive, paternalistic state.

ALTRUISM AND THE ALL-POWERFUL STATE

The rise of collectivism requires the inculcation of dependency. People must be led to believe that they are incapable of managing their lives by relying on their own judgment and their own actions. They must be made to conclude that they cannot fulfill their needs without the guidance, and the sacrifices, of others. They must come to feel perpetually indebted to the collective.

The welfare-regulatory state cultivates this state of mind.

To see how entrenched the idea of dependency has become, let's examine the ubiquitous admonition to "give something back." A member of a school board in Palm Beach, Florida, explaining why community service should be a requirement for high school graduation, declares: "We have a great deal of prosperity and wonderful things in this country, but for young people there isn't a strong sense of moral consciousness. There's not a sense of knowing what it means to give back to a community that gives you so much."[27] Billionaire Warren Buffett, announcing that he owes a debt to humanity for his "extraordinary good fortune," says: "I won what I call the ovarian lottery," since "the odds against my 1930 birth taking place in the U.S. were at least 30 to 1." In return, he and his family will "keep all we can conceivably need and distribute the rest to society, for its needs."[28] Whenever successful individuals donate their time or money to the needy, their explanation is that they are merely "giving back" some of what they have received. But exactly to whom and for what is this "repayment" being made?

When Warren Buffett gives away his money to treat the ill in Africa, are the recipients the ones who made him rich? When a high school student volunteers for the Salvation Army, is he helping the people responsible for his "prosperity and wonderful things"? He may owe gratitude to his parents, but why to the poor? Did they supply his education? Did they provide him with him his food, shelter and clothing? What is he giving *back* to them?

There are certainly things one obtains by virtue of living in a society rather than on some uninhabited island. But they are obtained by *trade*. And they are obtained from specific individuals. You may get a salary from your employer, a mortgage from a bank and a meal from a restaurant. What you owe them—and *only* them—is the fulfillment of your side of the exchange. You owe them, respectively, competent work, timely loan payments and the price of dinner. If you achieve success in a free society, you have worked for it. You have no cause for guilt over others' lack of success. You have given value for value in dealing with people. You have no unpaid debt to some amorphous community.

The one legitimate point raised by Buffett is that life is immeasurably better in the United States than in some dictatorship. In America, the individual is (relatively) free, while in many other countries he is a persecuted serf. So there is indeed a certain debt owed by every U.S. citizen. But it is an *intellectual* debt, and it is owed to the thinkers who made a nation of freedom and prosperity possible. The debt is to philosophers such as John Locke, who first identified the principle of individual rights. The debt is to America's Founding Fathers, who implemented that principle by creating the Declaration of Independence and the Constitution. But one does not show gratitude for these values by acting in contradiction to them. One does not salute the individual's inalienable right to the pursuit of his happiness by accepting a duty to sacrifice that happiness to the needs of others. One does not uphold the American ideal of individualism by espousing the tenets of collectivism.

If Buffett wants to make an appropriate gesture, he can donate his money to some educational institute that disseminates the principles of individualism and capitalism. What he is doing, though, is not "giving back," but giving *up*—he is repudiating those principles. He is accepting the view that the individual's achievements are never *earned*, but are only altruistic gifts from society. He is sanctioning the claim that one owes one's existence to the munificence of the collective.

Whom the collectivists would rule, they first make dependent. All elements of the welfare state reinforce the notion of the individual's helplessness. Over and over, people are told they cannot survive unless a vast, paternalistic government takes care of their needs. People come to believe that they are materially and intellectually dependent on the state—that it must provide them not only with their daily bread, but with the calculations for their daily allowable intake of carbohydrates. They come to believe that they are kept alive only through the sacrifices of others, and that they in turn must be willing to make the sacrifices society demands of them. They come to believe that the self-sustaining, self-reliant, self-responsible individual is a myth.

Once someone absorbs the notion of his basic impotence, he is primed to follow orders. A man waiting passively to be fed, clothed and housed is a man waiting compliantly to be told what he may eat, how he may dress and where he may reside. He is a man waiting to be told how, and whether, he may live.

Which paves the way for the totalitarian state.

Totalitarianism is the culmination of the creed of self-sacrifice. It allows no selfish values, no private profit, no individual rights. It is a system under which every shred of self-interest is ripped away from the individual, as all his energies, his plans and his aspirations are subordinated to the needs of the collective. As Karl Marx succinctly described the altruist morality behind the totalitarian state: "From each according to his ability, to each according to his need."

Taking their inspiration from Plato's all-knowing Philosopher-King, totalitarian rulers wield absolute power on the premise that they alone can fathom what is truly best for their subjects. A dictator is the paternalist-in-chief. Every aspect of people's lives, from the work they are told to perform to the opinions they are permitted to express, is rigidly controlled, so that everyone becomes a selfless slave of the state.

When the dictatorship in China compels a pregnant woman to undergo an abortion if she's already had one child, it is demanding that her interests be sacrificed to the needs of the nation. When the dictatorship in Iran stones to death people who have renounced Islam, it is demanding that they be sacrificed to the needs of Muslim society. When the dictatorship in the Soviet Union shipped political dissidents to Siberian gulags, it was demanding that they be sacrificed to the needs of the proletariat. When the dictatorship in Nazi Germany condemned Jews to the gas chambers, it was demanding that they be sacrificed to the needs of the Aryan race. These evils are all perpetrated in compliance with the dictum that the individual exists only to satisfy the demands of the collective.

Here, for example, is Adolf Hitler, explaining the philosophy behind Nazism:

> It is thus necessary that the individual should finally come to real-
> ize that his own ego is of no importance in comparison with the

existence of his nation; that the position of the individual ego is conditioned solely by the interests of the nation as a whole; . . . and that the higher interests involved in the life of the whole must here set the limits and lay down the duties of interests of the individual. . . . By this we understand only the individual's capacity to make sacrifices for the community, for his fellow men.[29]

Here is Lenin, explaining the philosophy behind Communism:

[F]or the sake of starting the world proletarian revolution, we cannot and must not hesitate to make the heaviest sacrifices.[30]

Here is Mao Tse-tung, explaining the same ideology:

[W]e Chinese Communists, who base all our actions on the highest interests of the broadest masses of the Chinese people and who are fully convinced of the justice of our cause, never balk at any personal sacrifice and are ready at all times to give our lives for the cause.[31]

It does not matter whether a dictator genuinely believes in altruism or is just an opportunistic power-luster. The point is that altruism provides the *moral sanction* for his rule. Tanks and machine guns alone do not sustain a dictatorship. Dictators could not maintain power if they announced that they were running their countries for their personal enrichment. Unlike the common crook—who does not proclaim that crime is a virtue, but rather does his wrongdoing by stealth and hopes to escape notice—the dictator publicly declares that his actions are *good* for the nation. This is why massive, unrelenting propaganda is so indispensable to despots. They realize that they must try to justify their reign. And they do so by invoking the precepts of self-sacrifice.

The premise that one's "own ego is of no importance in comparison with the existence of his nation" is what generates collaboration by the people necessary to the functioning of a dictatorship—from those who man the tanks and the machine guns, to those who operate the assorted ministries, to those who churn out the books and the movies glorifying the political system, to those who dutifully inform on "enemies of the state," to those who simply suspend judgment by telling themselves: "Who am I to know better?" The dictator's subjects, whether high officials or lowly peons, are continually urged to sacrifice for the collective. They are enjoined to forsake their own interests, to suppress personal desires, to meld with the group, to refrain from complaining, to have faith in the master plan. The misery, the torture and the killing—they are repeatedly assured—are all for the sake of a "greater good."

The more vigorously a dictator espouses an ideology of collectivism, the more admirable he becomes to the rest of the world, regardless of how much blood he spills. Even critics of the Soviet Union, the most murderous dictatorship in modern history, often characterized it as pursuing an idealistic, albeit impractical, goal. As one U.S. diplomat, known for his anti-communism, said of Marxism: "I think it's probably the most noble and unselfish ideology that's been devised since Christianity. It just doesn't work."[32]

But in a totalitarian state the people are ordered to *make* the unworkable work. They are told that the system's failures are a result of their unwillingness to eradicate all traces of selfishness from their minds. They are urged to renounce their own happiness for the "higher good" of serving the collective. They are assured that if they surrender their egos and embrace the ruler's edicts, a Workers' Paradise or a thousand-year Reich will emerge. They are instructed not to question, but to obey. And most of the population, actively or passively, acquiesces.

Dictatorships do not sprout at random. They grow only in fertile soil. They develop in one country, but cannot in another, because they need a culture in which dependency has fully taken root. A dictatorship requires a citizenry of docile souls and pliable minds. It requires people who have been steeped in a philosophy of self-sacrifice and self-abnegation. It requires people who believe they have a duty to place themselves at the disposal of the state. It requires people who wish to be led. It requires people whose response to commands is the equivalent of a deferential "Heil Hitler."

It requires people who are willing to submit.

Many of Russia's citizens, for example, even after the collapse of Communism, still idolize Lenin and Stalin and still welcome authoritarian rule.

Rudolf Hoess, the Nazi commandant of the Auschwitz concentration camp, approvingly described this psychology:

Every German had to subordinate himself unquestioningly and uncritically to the leaders of the State, who alone were in a position to understand the real needs of the people and to direct them along the right path.[33]

No tyrant can enslave a people who genuinely value freedom. This is why a dictatorship cannot arise in America—at least not yet. The mentality required is the diametric opposite of the one that founded this country.

The United States was born of a radical spirit of individualism. Its citizens were declared to be independent, sovereign individuals with inalienable rights. Each person was to be an end in himself, with the government serving as his agent. The attitude of submissiveness was repudiated. The newly emerging view of man, as presented by Thomas Jefferson, was that "the mass of mankind has not been born with saddles on their backs, nor a favored few booted and spurred, ready to ride them."[34] Each man's life was to be his own, not the state's. It was an outlook that upheld, not self-sacrifice, but the pursuit of happiness—not dependency and a nanny-state, but self-esteem and limited government. This mindset was expressed in such popular demands as "Don't tread on me" and "Give me liberty or give me death." It is a mindset very different from that reflected in such contemporary demands as "Don't cut my welfare benefits" or "Give me free health care."

But the spirit of early America, which remained strong through the nineteenth century, now seems eons removed from us. It is difficult to conceive, for example, that a U.S. president actually vetoed a bill to fund mental asylums, stating: "I cannot find any authority in the Constitution for making the federal government the great almoner of public charity." Such legislation, President Franklin Pierce said in 1854, would be "subversive of the whole theory upon which the Union of these States is founded."[35] That is, it would undermine the principle that the function of government is not to compel some people to sacrifice for others, but to protect the individual rights of all.

Although America was established on that principle, a contradiction was present from the start. The Founders erected a glorious political structure to secure our liberty, but did not realize that its foundation—its code of morality—was flawed. They *implicitly* embraced the ideas of egoism, while *explicitly* they accepted the tenets of altruism. By upholding individual liberty, they tacitly endorsed the egoist idea that man is an end in himself. But when directly addressing the question of what constitutes the good, they generally believed that to be moral is to serve the needs of others. For example, Thomas Jefferson, who rejected the supernaturalism of the Bible, nonetheless regarded the altruistic teachings of Jesus as "the most sublime and benevolent code of morals which has ever been offered to man."[36] Holding an innocently benign interpretation of altruism, the Founders did not understand its full ramifications. They did not realize that the view of man as a free, autonomous being would ultimately be nullified by the view of man as his brother's keeper. Over time, however, the contradiction unfolded.

The result was a slow, steady erosion of the meaning and the accomplishments of the American Revolution. The rights of the individual kept shrinking and the reach of the state kept expanding. Government budgets grew, agencies grew, taxation grew, regulations grew, the power of the collective grew. We are now a nation that is, precariously, part free and part statist. And it all began with the premise that everyone has a duty to sacrifice for the needy. And it will all end—unless that premise is challenged—with the complete disappearance of our freedom. The fabric that makes up the welfare state's "safety net" will eventually become the material for the suffocating straitjacket of the omnipotent state.

The road to hell is indeed paved with good intentions—but only when "good" is defined by the standard of altruism.

SEVEN

THE BLACK HOLE
OF SELFLESSNESS

MOST PEOPLE THINK THAT THE SELFLESS PERSON GIVES
up his wealth but holds tightly to his own ideas. They believe that
he forms strong, unyielding views and lives by what he judges to be
true. But they are mistaken. The truly selfless individual is permitted no personal convictions.

Altruism demands that you sacrifice not just your material assets
but your intellectual ones as well. It is the people in need who are
given the right to decide how you should dispose of whatever you
possess, whether it resides in your wallet or in your brain.

Altruism demands the sacrifice of the *mind*.

HUMAN COGNITION: A SUPREMELY SELFISH ACT

The ethics of altruism requires you to give away what you value. But
every act of evaluation—of classifying something as a value—is an

act of cognition. It is an act of grasping a certain relationship. It is an identification of the fact that something relates to your life in a positive way—that it is *good* for you—and that you should therefore seek to gain it. And when you sacrifice a value, you sacrifice that identification. You surrender the cognitive conclusion that the thing in question *is* a value. When you judge that it is good for you to have something, altruism says *no*—you must instead accept the judgment that it is "good" for you to give it up.

The altruist doctrine seeks to set the cognitive terms not only for what is to be regarded as good, but for what is to be regarded as true. When the FDA, for example, exercises its monopoly power to approve or reject a drug, it establishes, by political fiat, what is and is not to be considered a fact of medical science. A drug may actually benefit you but, if it is deemed detrimental to the needs of the collective, you are ordered to act on the premise that the drug is detrimental to you.

This type of control extends into the realm of ideas. A pharmaceutical manufacturer, for instance, faces restrictions not only on selling a drug for a use unacceptable to the FDA, but even on showing doctors medical literature that contradicts the agency's position.[1]

According to altruism, we must adapt our perception of reality to accommodate the needs of others. We must not endorse ideas that the needy find objectionable. Thus, guards at a maximum-security prison in Canada were forbidden to wear stab-proof vests because, a prison official explained, "If you have that kind of presence symbolized by [a stab-proof vest], you're sending a signal to the prisoner that you consider him to be a dangerous person."[2] A U.S. publisher of reading tests for schoolchildren rejected a proposed passage about a blind man's courageous hike to the top of Mount McKinley because "it suggested that people who are blind are somehow at a disadvantage compared to people who have normal sight."[3] The history department in a British secondary school excluded the Holocaust as a topic for coursework "for fear of confronting anti-Semitic sentiment and Holocaust denial among some Muslim pupils."[4] This is all altruism at work. It is altruism telling us that we must sacrifice what we regard as the truth. If the deprived feel the need to hold a certain idea, we must oblige them, even if we know the idea is false. We must, in effect, communicate to the ignorant that the Holocaust is a myth; to the blind that one can climb mountains as easily without the faculty sight as with it; and to imprisoned murderers that we consider them unthreatening.

And if the needy are to determine what thoughts we may communicate, why shouldn't they determine what thoughts we may form in the first place? I discussed in Chapter 3 how, under altruism, the needs of others must take precedence over one's own moral principles. Now we can see how this precedence applies to *all* of one's convictions. At the core of selfishness is the exercise of an independent mind. You reach a conclusion when *you* have determined that it is valid. You decide that 2 + 2 = 4, not because of public opinion, but because *you* have grasped that it is true. Cognition is a selfish process. But if selfishness is to be repudiated, you must abdicate this process. You must grant a non-you the final say in reaching cognitive verdicts. For your consciousness to function selflessly, it must be driven by the views of others.

The fully selfless man thus harbors no personal convictions. Just as his standard of the good is whatever others want, his standard of the true is whatever others believe. He does nothing that will elicit people's disagreement. He is driven by *their* needs, *their* wishes, *their* demands, *their* ideas. In both thought and action, he is their deferential servant.

The sacrifice of one's mind is entailed in the very method by which anyone accepts the altruist code. As discussed earlier, since there is no earthly reason for one man to subordinate his life to another, the person who espouses self-sacrifice does so on faith. He believes in altruism because his authorities—his mother, his pastor, his teachers, the social consensus—have declared it to be indisputable. Reason is the means by which an individual controls the workings of his mind and guides the course of his life. Faith, however, is the means by which he relinquishes control. Faith is the suspension of his rational faculty. Faith is the means by which he selflessly allows others to shape his thoughts and rule his life.

And there is a supplementary target in this attack on the self. Concomitant with the demand to sacrifice your mind is the demand to sacrifice your self-esteem.

Don't take pride in yourself, we are regularly instructed—be humble. Don't be self-assertive—be self-deprecating. Don't seek your happiness—you exist only to serve. Don't think your life is something precious—it's just sacrificial fodder. Don't think you're good—deep down, no one is any good.

The traditional form of this message comes mainly from Christianity, which tells us that we are all incurably defiled by Original Sin. In the words of the medieval Pope Innocent III: "Man is made of mud and ashes. . . . Why are you proud, O mud? Wherefore are thou exalted? What are you, O ash, that you should boast? . . . O the vile ignobility of human existence!"[5] Similarly, in the contemporary language of Reverend Billy Graham: "You can break down and thresh out and destroy every mountain of self and every obstacle in your way, if you will just be a worm. . . . A worm is perfectly helpless. It has no strength to fight or protect itself from danger. Whether food for birds or to be trampled underfoot by man, it resigns itself to sacrifice. . . . It lives entirely for others. . . . [L]earn the lesson of the worm and humble yourself before God."[6] As mandated by the egalitarian dictates of the Sermon on the Mount, you must "love your enemies, bless them that curse you, do good to them that hate you, and pray for them which despitefully use you and persecute you."[7] If we are all equally hopeless sinners by God's standards, everyone must regard himself as no better than the most despicable degenerate.

The more avant-garde form of this message comes from modern intellectuals, who tell us that man is an insignificant piece of protoplasm—that he resides in a senseless universe—that his life has no meaning or purpose—that rationality is a mirage, volition a fiction, achievement a delusion. Their updated version of the Sermon on the

Mount is a more nihilistic egalitarianism, one in which there are no standards of judgment at all, not even God's.

We are all equal, our foremost intellectuals say—by which they mean: we are equally worthless. There are no admirable people, only flawed ones. There are no heroes, only folks with clay feet. The *anti*-hero is the star in modern literature and theater. Idealism is something one is supposed to outgrow upon entering adulthood. To aspire is to be naïve. Depictions of man as noble elicit condescending sneers from our cultural critics. The policies of our social leaders are designed to cut people down, to keep anyone from thinking he is *good*. The diligent high school student, who is proud that he has achieved top grades, is compelled to spend his time scouring bedpans if he wants a diploma. The successful entrepreneur, who is proud that he has created vast wealth, is told that he must acknowledge the primacy of society by "giving back" what he has acquired.

No one—according to the dominant philosophy of our age—is entitled to esteem himself. We must therefore stop making differentiations among people. Are there disparities in the incomes people earn? Eliminate them. Are there disparities in the abilities people possess? Ignore them. Are there disparities in the validity of various beliefs people hold? Treat them all the same: no one can claim to know what is true.

As is the case with altruists' broader denunciation of selfishness, their assault on self-esteem is abetted by a policy of obfuscation. They try to disguise the true nature of what they are condemning by concocting a straw man. So they portray self-esteem as something pitiable—as exemplified by the posturing braggart, desperate to impress an audience with his exaggerated accomplishments. Or they portray it as something dangerous—as exemplified by the volatile, hair-trigger personality, who is so obsessed with his fragile "ego" that he reacts violently to any slight. Or they portray it as something trivial and arbitrary—as exemplified by many of today's kindergarteners, who are taught that anyone can manufacture a sense of self-worth by mindlessly chanting "I am special."

But none of these depictions represents genuine self-esteem. The purveyors of altruism do not want us to learn that self-esteem is *earned*—that it is based on the character one has actually achieved and not on the mantras one spouts or on the flattery one wheedles from others. Authentic self-esteem derives from an honest, independent assessment of oneself. It is the psychological confirmation that one is living up to one's own, rational standards. As Aristotle said: "Pride, then, seems to be a sort of crown of the virtues; for it makes them greater, and it is not found without them. Therefore, it is hard to be truly proud; for it is impossible without nobility and goodness of character."[8] A man of self-esteem is secure in his own judgment of himself. He does not feel fundamentally threatened by someone else's criticism. Only the "other-ist" orientation of altruism could give rise to the notion that self-worth hinges on the opinions of one's neighbors.

Genuine self-esteem is an aspect of genuine selfishness. Ayn Rand described pride as "moral ambitiousness,"[9] requiring a "radiant selfishness of soul which desires the best in all things, in values of matter and spirit."[10] Self-esteem is embodied in the man who has shaped his character into one that *deserves* the happiness he seeks to achieve. It is embodied in the man who is confident in his ability to be the master of his own existence and who deems himself worthy of the continuous effort that life requires. The man of self-esteem indignantly rejects the role of sacrificial animal, while the man lacking self-esteem readily accepts it.

Selfishness requires courage. It takes inner strength to establish one's goals and to fight to attain them. It takes steadfast resolve to hold onto one's values and principles in the face of the obstacles one inevitably encounters. It takes an enduring commitment to battle for one's happiness and to refuse to settle for less than what is possible.

Selflessness, by contrast, is the state of giving up.

Selflessness is the belief that one's own happiness is unimportant, because one's own life is unimportant. The selfless man does not seek anything that gives him pleasure—that would be selfish. Indeed, if he finds that he takes joy in some activity, even the activity of helping others, it means that he is not sacrificing enough and that he has still more of himself to relinquish. If he is happy in giving away half his wealth, he must do more. He must give until the giving makes him suffer, so that he is being truly selfless. His life must consist in fulfilling burdensome duties, not pursuing passionate values. He can have no real values—except the "value" of surrendering his values.

Love, according to the platitudes of altruism, is supposed to be the basic solution to our problems. But the truly selfless man is incapable even of that value. As Howard Roark remarks in *The Fountainhead:* "To say 'I love you' one must know first how to say the 'I.'"[11]

Selflessness is not a positive state. It is a vacuum. The selfless man has given up the responsibility of thinking—of choosing, of learning, of creating, of valuing. He lives not just *for* others, but *through* others. He does not ask himself: "What do I think is true? What do I think I should do?" Instead, he asks: "What do others believe? What do others desire of me?" He is an empty vessel, waiting to be filled by the effluent flowing from other people. The irony is that the selfless man—the man who gives away the pieces of his life for the sake of others—is actually a parasite: he is abjectly dependent on others to supply him with the contents of his consciousness.

THE ZOMBIE ORDER-FOLLOWERS

The phenomenon of selflessness explains seemingly mystifying acts of destructiveness. Consider three examples.

In the bizarre 1978 mass-suicide at Jonestown, over nine hundred Americans swallowed cyanide-laced fruit punch at the behest of their leader, Jim Jones. They were members of the "People's Temple" commune in Guyana, having emigrated from California to establish a socialist utopia. Many signed over to Jones their homes, their belongings, their Social Security checks, even custody of their children. They took their orders from him and called him "Dad." Told that the outside world wanted to destroy their way of life, they held rehearsals for the suicide ritual. And when Jones—fearing a U.S. investigation of his activities—announced that the time had come, they compliantly drank their Kool-Aid (with the adults administering the poison to some 150 infants and children under the age of eleven).[12]

Why did they do it? A journalist who was present at the time, and who subsequently wrote a book about Jonestown, offered in an interview this description of Jones's followers:

> The people who were attracted to the Temple did, for the most part, have one common trait. They were altruistic. . . . They had a need to join an organization where they were doing something meaningful. Keep in mind that this was in the post-civil rights and post-Vietnam eras, and a lot of young people, in particular, and older ones, too, were looking for some outlet for their desire to do things for their fellow man.[13]

Then there is the current scourge of Islamist suicide-bombers. The people who are willing to destroy themselves in order to take their victims with them are acting selflessly. They dutifully blow up children in school buses because their authorities inform them that they are bringing about a "greater good." Their mullahs promise them that their community will be grateful, and their imams inform them that they are doing Allah's will.

And then there are the unspeakable atrocities of Nazism. Adolf Eichmann, the man appointed to oversee the eradication of the Jews, explained afterward how he approached his task:

From my childhood, obedience was something I could not get out of my system. . . . It was unthinkable that I would not follow orders. . . . Now that I look back, I realize that a life predicated on being obedient and taking orders is a very comfortable life indeed. Living in such a way reduces to a minimum one's own need to think.[14]

This attitude pervaded the Nazi ranks, from bottom to top. In a postwar interview a soldier stationed at a concentration camp was asked whether he had ever felt compassion for the prisoners there. He replied: "Yes . . . but I had to overcome it. That was the sacrifice I had to make for the greater cause."[15] The commandant of the Auschwitz camp, Rudolf Hoess, expressed the same idea with regard to his being instructed to commence the killings: "I did not reflect on it at the time. I had been given an order and I had to carry it out. Whether this mass extermination of the Jews was necessary or not was something on which I could not allow myself to form an opinion."[16]

Such people, in all such cases, come as close as possible to achieving full selflessness. They share one dominant characteristic: a refusal to activate their minds. The only way for them not to comprehend the evil they perpetrate is to suspend their power of comprehension. They simply blank out. They believe in self-sacrifice, and what they sacrifice first is their rational faculty. They engage in no independent judgment. All these selfless destroyers recoil from the selfish act of *thinking*. Instead, they allow their minds to be molded by the assertions of others—whether a socialist leader, a Muslim cleric or a Nazi Fuhrer. They become zombies, pliant obeyers who willingly commit the most abominable crimes. They insistently tell themselves that as long as they are being assured that their actions are righteous, who are they to form a dissenting viewpoint?

The essence of this mentality is best expressed in a pithy statement by Hermann Goering, founder of the Nazi Gestapo, in defense of Hitler's economic policies: "I tell you, if the Fuhrer wishes it, then two times two are five."[17]

That represents the lethal void of selflessness.

EIGHT

THE GOAL OF SELF-SACRIFICE

ALTRUISM'S PROPONENTS EXHIBIT VARYING DEGREES OF understanding of their creed. At the more innocent end of this spectrum are the people who uncritically believe that some of us must be sacrificed so that others, or "society as a whole," can benefit. But those at the opposite end—the theorists and intellectuals of altruism, the ones who grasp the full implication of the altruist code, the avid leaders as against passive followers, the pushers rather than just the users—have a very different motivation. They advocate self-sacrifice, not as a means of benefiting anyone—but as an end in itself.

THE ALTRUISTIC ENVIERS

We're familiar with the ugly phenomenon of envy. There are people who resent the fact that a neighbor has a bigger house or that a co-worker receives a promotion. These enviers feel a secret delight in contemplating the possibility that the neighbor will be unable to meet his mortgage payments and will have his house repossessed, or that the co-worker will do badly in his new position and will be fired. It is not that the enviers want to acquire a better house or a better job; they simply want those who *have* acquired it to lose it. They do not seek success for themselves—they seek failure for others.

The same is true of altruism's zealous pushers. When they urge self-sacrifice, their ultimate goal is not for the recipients to gain—but for the donors to lose.

Consider the policy, discussed in Chapter 1, under which high school students are required to perform community service as a condition for graduating. What is the purpose of this policy? If students care for patients at a hospital, for example, their efforts qualify. But students are not permitted to pay people—say, people professionally trained in health care—to provide the same service, even if doing so would be far better for the patients. Nor can students fulfill their requirements if *they* are paid by the hospital for their work. They may be assisting in the hospital's most promising cancer research, but if they are doing so for pay, their efforts will not meet the necessary criteria. The student, according to one school's guidelines, may not "stand to gain personally" and must perform "service to the community with no expectation of reward or even thanks."[1] That is, the measure of diploma-worthiness is the degree of a student's willingness to sacrifice, not the degree of help he actually provides to others.

Or consider all the praise bestowed upon Mother Teresa for comforting the sick and the dying, or upon the Peace Corps for distributing food and toiletries to impoverished villages in Africa. In contrast, profit-seeking corporations that have alleviated world suffering through such advances as antibiotics, anesthetics, vaccines and contraceptives, or that have drastically reduced world hunger through such innovations as high-yielding, genetically modified crops, are scorned as exploitative money-chasers.

The altruist dispenses moral approval in proportion to the loss suffered by the sacrificer, not to any putative gains enjoyed by the recipient. In the arch-example of selflessness, the Bible's Abraham is hailed for being ready to kill his son Isaac simply because God commanded it. Abraham is venerated for his subservience, for being willing to surrender his most cherished value, even though there was plainly no benefit to anyone—not to Abraham's family, not to his community, not even to God—in having Isaac dead. It is the sheer act of self-sacrifice, performed for its own sake, that so enamors the altruist.

When altruists campaign against income inequality, it is not the poor they want to lift up as much as it is the rich they want to drag down. They display no moral indignation if everyone is equally impoverished. To the contrary, socialist countries elicit the altruists' admiration, despite the fact that virtually everyone's standard of living there is far inferior to that of the West's poorest populations. On the other hand, if the lives of the West's poor improve, but the lives of the rich improve more, the altruists express outrage. For instance, a newspaper story carries the headline "Nation's Wealth Disparity

Widens," and begins: "The gaps in wealth between the rich and the poor . . . have grown wider, the Federal Reserve said. . . . The difference in median net wealth between the 10 percent of families with the highest incomes and the 20 percent of families with the lowest incomes jumped 70 percent." It is not until the ninth paragraph of this fifteen-paragraph story that we learn the following salient fact: "Net worth for the lowest income group . . . *rose 25 percent to $7,900.*"[2] (Emphasis added.)

To a rational person, the fact that his wealth increases is something good. To the altruist, however, it becomes something deplorable if others' wealth increases faster. If we are all leveled, if no one is permitted to be better off than the most destitute among us, then the mandate of altruism is being fulfilled. But if any inequality exists, it means the "haves" are failing to sacrifice sufficiently. So the altruist intervenes to prevent anyone from rising much above his brethren. He insists that those too far from the bottom must be sacrificed. Wealth becomes a sign of culpability and a cause for punishment. The altruist condemns the users of limousines and penthouse suites, he inveighs against high salaries and corporate bonuses, he demands—as one Congressional bill proposed—that there be a limit to how much higher an executive's compensation can be than that of the company's lowest-paid worker.[3]

Some cultures, of course, display this type of envy far more openly than others. In Finland, for example, traffic fines are assessed in proportion to the offender's income. One wealthy motorist there was stopped for driving 43 miles per hour in a 25-miles-per-hour zone. The police officer took the driver's social security number, used a cell phone to instantly access the man's tax returns—and issued him a ticket for $71,000! "This is a Nordic tradition," said an official of the Ministry of Interior. "We have progressive taxation and progressive punishments. So the more you earn, the more you pay."[4]

In an effort to make semi-plausible their hostility toward the rich, altruists claim that one person's enrichment causes another person's impoverishment. But in a free market, an increase in wealth has the opposite effect. In a free market, wealth is not some fixed, unchangeable quantity. Rather, an individual's wealth is *created*. It is not forcibly taken from others; it is something that did not exist before. Those whose limited ability allows them to earn less only benefit from those able to earn more. How did the richest people become rich? By producing the goods—the cars, the houses, the airplanes, the computers, the smartphones—that enhance the lives of us all. Those who produce more earn more, and those who produce less earn less. But all gain when production is unfettered. When the most capable are able to dine on filet mignon, the least capable are able to eat hamburger—as against the menu of gruel, or of starvation, that awaits everybody under egalitarianism.

When wealth is redistributed everyone's standard of living is ultimately lowered. Redistribution amounts to a one-time consumption of *productive capital*—the equivalent of confiscating a thriving factory, dismantling it and selling the bricks to pay for unemployment benefits. Once the factory stops functioning, and the bricks have run out, what then will sustain the "have-nots"?

Of course, if people grow rich by means of special favors from government, then their wealth *does* come out of the pockets of the non-favored. In that case, though, the proper object of condemnation is not the rich or the system of capitalism—but the influence-peddling inherent in a non-capitalist system (including America's current mixed economy). When the government altruistically manages the economy on behalf of an ineffable public interest, cronyism inevitably emerges as pressure groups vie to be considered the public. But when laws objectively define and safeguard individual rights, the government has no power to dole out favors and there is no influence to be peddled.

The assault on income inequality, like other altruist campaigns, reflects not a justified anger against the recipients of government privileges, but the envier's resentment toward those who have earned what he hasn't. It reflects the desire to "cut down the tall poppies," i.e., to sacrifice the successful simply because they have succeeded while others haven't.

A CODE OF DISVALUES

This motivation is not a deviation from, but is implicit in, the doctrine of altruism. It is implicit in the way altruism defines the good—or rather, in the way it *defaults* on defining the good.

A code of ethics is supposed to identify good and bad, benefit and harm. Religion, for example, holds that to achieve the good is to obey God's commandments—which means that those who do so benefit in some way, while those who rely instead on their own judgment are harming themselves. Rational egoism, to take an opposite example, holds that to achieve the good is to adopt a life of reason, independence and productiveness—which means that those who do so benefit, while those who live irrationally and become dependent moochers are harmed.

What constitutes the good according to altruism? When you ask: "By what principle should I lead my life?" the altruist answers: "You should do, not what is good for you, but what is good for your neighbor." But what *is* the good of your neighbor? Well, it's whatever is good for *his* neighbor, which is whatever is good for *his* neighbor, which is. . . . Altruism declares that you benefit by benefiting someone other than yourself. And how does *that* person benefit? By benefiting someone other than himself, who benefits by. . . .

The ethics of altruism fails to offer a genuine conception of the good. It defines the good not by the nature of your actions, but by the fact that the intended beneficiary is non-you rather than you. The only meaning that can be attached to the idea of "good" or "benefit," therefore, is the act of self-sacrifice itself. The sheer act of sacrificing, not any positive consequences for others, is the essence of the good according to altruism.

Keep in mind that sacrificing means giving up something of value to you for something that isn't. If you are a student who chooses to study for a crucial exam rather than spend all night at a fraternity party, you are not sacrificing; you are benefiting. But if you choose to jeopardize your education by attending the party in order to satisfy some great-aunt's desire to have you show off the socks she has knitted for you, then you *are* sacrificing; you are accepting a duty to harm yourself for the sake of others. To declare that self-sacrifice is beneficial to you is to declare that you somehow benefit by sacrificing what you know will benefit you. In other words, the good, in altruism's convoluted view, is that which harms you!

A code of ethics is supposed to be a set of basic values—a guide to what you should pursue, a standard for what you should act to attain. Altruism fails in this task. It does not identify the values you should seek. It tells you only what to renounce. Altruism does not instruct you to achieve, say, happiness, or knowledge or wealth—or even poverty. When it directs you to give away your money, it does not direct you to hold poverty as a value. The code of asceticism, by way of contrast, *does* value poverty. But if you become an ardent ascetic and disdain earthly goods, if you seek only "spiritual transcendence" and are willing to discard all your material possessions, you get no moral credit from altruism for handing them over to the poor. To receive such credit, you have to *value* those goods. You have to desire them, you have to prize them, you have to yearn to use them in furtherance of your own life—and then make the sacrifice of giving them away. You must be willing to suffer, with the degree of your pain being the measure of your virtue.

Altruism is a code of *dis*values. It leeches off your pre-existing values and tells you, in effect: "Whatever you have chosen to value, surrender it." From your bank account to your political convictions, from your transplantable organs to your moral integrity—if it is important to you, you must give it up for the sake of other people. The highest value, according to altruism, is . . . to give up your highest values.

The philosopher Immanuel Kant, a champion of the ethics of self-sacrifice, presents the issue starkly. He says that the very choice to live should be made, not out of any personal desire for life, but rather as an unchosen, onerous, selfless duty. Because most people find value in living, he says, "the maxim of doing so [i.e., of keeping oneself alive] has no moral import." If, however, "adversities and hopeless sorrow completely take away the relish for life, if an unfortunate man, strong in soul, is indignant rather than despondent or dejected over his fate and wishes for death, and yet preserves his life without loving it and from neither inclination [i.e., desire] nor fear but from duty—then his maxim has a moral import."[5] In other words, if you act out of a duty to embrace a non-value—if you choose to continue living *because* life holds no benefit for you, *because* life means agony—only then are you being virtuous.

This approach to ethics is used to justify the worst actions of the enviers and haters. It is used by those who want to destroy not just some particular value, such as high incomes, but the achievement—and the achievers—of *any* value. To value something is to elevate it above a non-value. The egalitarian levelers wish to do away with all such differentiations.

Do you, for instance, regard beauty as something good? The egalitarians vilify the admiration of beauty in people. They want equal time for the ugly. They deplore the prevalence of attractive newscasters, pretty dolls, glamorous models and beauty contests. They condemn it all as discriminatory "lookism."

Do you admire eloquent speech? The egalitarians declare that oratory contests, which are designed to display speaking skills, should include deaf-mutes communicating through sign language—an arrangement that serves only to undermine the value of oratorical ability.[6] They revile what they call "ableism," defined as "the oppression of the differently abled by the temporarily abled."[7] To value *any* ability someone possesses—they believe—is to oppress all who lack it.

Do you think that a society of reason, science and freedom is better than one of superstition, witch-doctory and slavery? The egalitarians want to prevent our schoolteachers from conveying such non-egalitarian value-judgments to students. Instead—as one state law asserts—students must be taught to "understand that a specific culture is not intrinsically superior or inferior to another."[8]

Even such seemingly self-evident values as health become targets of the value-haters. For example, some people suffer from autism, which involves a malfunction of the brain. The condition first shows up in the very young. Severely autistic children have trouble forming words, they are unable to understand or respond to communication from others, they become fixated on various objects, they go into terrible tantrums. Their cognitive apparatus is highly defective. It is a nightmare existence for the parents, who try desperately to get the child's mind to operate properly.

But there is a "neurodiversity" movement that wants all curative efforts to cease. This movement, according to a *New York Times* article, "is rooted in a view of autism as an alternative form of brain wiring, with its own benefits and drawbacks, rather than a devastating disorder in need of curing."[9] There is no better or worse, the egalitarian avers—there is only "different." Wikipedia reports that members of various "autism rights" organizations "view autism as a way of life rather than as a disease and thus advocate acceptance over a search for a cure. . . . The anti-cure perspective endorsed by the movement is a view that autism is not a disorder, but a normal occurrence." One of the movement's leaders, Wikipedia continues, "argues that autism is essential to a person, not a disease secondary to the person. . . . Visions for a future where autism has been eradicated, he believes, [are] the desire to end the autistic culture[!]"[10] So someone who seeks to heal the victims of autism is guilty of "ableism," of arrogantly making the judgment that living without a crushing disability is better than living with it.

The deaf face a similar movement. A surgical procedure called a cochlear implant can cure deafness in certain cases. But non-deaf parents who decide to have their children undergo the procedure are being denounced. "I think it is wrong for a hearing parent to deny a deaf child their cultural identity and force them to be hearing," says the editor of *Silent News,* a periodical published for the deaf.[11] An article in the *Atlantic* magazine, titled "Deafness as Culture," elaborates: "Deafness is not a disability. Instead, many deaf people now proclaim, they are a subculture like any other . . . and are no more in need of a cure for their condition than are Haitians or Hispanics."[12]

Medical professionals obviously find this view appalling. One such individual, the director of a hearing-research laboratory at Louisiana State University, voiced a resolute dissent: "[N]obody can make me say that a pathological cochlea is acceptable and should be allowed to continue to exist as long as I can do something about it. I am dedicated to curing deafness. That puts me on a collision course with those who are culturally deaf. That is interpreted as genocide of the deaf."[13]

In this battle, he has reason and justice on his side—but his opponents have altruism. The desire that one's deaf child should be able to hear is dismissed as selfish, while the desire of the deaf community to embrace its identity of deafness is venerated as a collective need. And the selfish must always sacrifice for the needy. As the editors of *Deaf Life* magazine declare: "An implant is the ultimate denial of deafness, the ultimate refusal to let deaf children be Deaf."[14] And that is perfectly true—it is a refusal to make the non-value of deafness equivalent to the value of hearing. It is a refusal to embrace the crippling ideology of egalitarianism.

Life requires us to make continual discriminations. We must discriminate between food and poison, health and sickness, intelligence and stupidity, an honest man and a thief. Obviously, some types of discrimination are irrational. Racial discrimination, for instance, is unjustified because in fact race does not determine character or abilities. But the egalitarians want us to treat *all* discriminations as invalid, regardless of whether or not they are based on fact. They try to smear every act of discrimination as the equivalent of racism.

They want us to believe that the evil of racial discrimination lies not in the racism, but in the act of discrimination as such. They insist that *nothing*—whether stemming from individual choice or natural endowment—should be deemed superior to anything else. Their goal is not to improve the lives of the non-rich, the non-beautiful, the non-healthy, the non-able—but to destroy the rich, the beautiful, the healthy, the able. More precisely, they seek to destroy the *value* of wealth, beauty, health and ability, by preventing anyone from benefiting from them. Which is accomplished by making the haves—i.e., those who possess anything of genuine value—sacrifice for the have-nots.

Sacrifice yourself—the egalitarians exhort—to the least deserving. After all, true sacrifice is the surrender of the best to the worst. Sacrifice your ambitions and your talents to the unambitious and the incompetent. Stop clinging to selfishness. Give away your money to those whose need consists of the desire, not to become rich, but for you to become poor. Sacrifice your autistic child's cure to the needs of the "autistic culture"—to its need, that is, to repudiate the value of a rationally functioning mind. Sacrifice that which promotes life to that which destroys it.

ANTI-LIFE

I've argued that the pushers of altruism are concerned with the act of self-sacrifice itself, not with any benefit accruing to the recipient. I've argued that by the standard of altruism, the very concept of "benefit" is indefinable. But if we bypass that irrational standard, is there *in fact* any benefit? A code of altruism clearly harms the people who make the sacrifices. But does it improve the lives of those who receive the sacrifices?

No. In the long run, it harms them too.

Altruism upholds parasitism. It declares that if anyone desires something he lacks, he is morally entitled to make others supply him with it. Altruism declares that mooching is moral but independence and self-reliance are not, that living off others is respectable but providing for oneself is crudely venal.

Nature, however, does not allow effortless living. It requires productiveness. It does not permit consumption without prior production. *Someone* must make the effort to create the goods on which every individual's life depends. When people trade the efforts of their labor with one another, production is advanced and their survival is safeguarded. But the parasite, who tries to live by obtaining the unearned, only undermines the conditions required for his own well-being.

The code of self-sacrifice destroys the producers. When they are told that they have a duty to sustain the non-producers, that the effort must be theirs but the rewards are to be distributed to others, that the harder they work, the more they will lose—what incentive do they have to continue to expend their energy? What is their motive to keep generating the goods, if the code ruling their lives is "from each according to his ability, to each according to his need"?

Altruism systematically drains the lifeblood from the very people on whom dependents depend.

And, in a deeper respect, it drains the lifeblood directly from the dependents themselves.

People often bemoan the fact that welfare programs discourage self-responsibility. This effect, however, is not an unfortunate by-product, but an essential element, of altruism. The consistent message delivered by the advocates of altruism is that sustaining your life is not your responsibility. Their message is that others have a duty to take care of you and that you are *owed* this care. Food, clothing, housing, cell phones, health insurance—if you need it, others have a duty to supply you with it. Why then should you make an effort to improve the circumstances of your life? You need not concern yourself with searching for a job, paying for your education, finding an apartment you can afford, learning new skills or moving to a different location where your opportunities are better. You have no moral obligation to do any of this, according to altruism. To the contrary, you should stay in public housing, you should stay on food stamps, you should stay on unemployment benefits—you should stay *dependent*. Indeed, how can the ethics of altruism be implemented unless people remain dependent on the sacrifices of others?

To live is to engage in self-generated action. It is an active process of attaining your values, a process that is not only a means but an end—a process not only of making life possible but of *living* it. Life *is* the actions we take to advance our existence. Altruism, however, calls for the opposite. It demands passivity. It enjoins you to withdraw from the pursuit of values and to have others engage in that pursuit for you. It urges you to have others care for you, which ultimately means: to have others *live* for you.

Imagine someone who fully embraces this idea. Imagine that he surrenders himself completely to the custody of others (who concomitantly accept an altruistic duty to oversee his needs). They take paternalistic charge of his life, while he does nothing for himself. They choose his food and feed him, they choose his clothing and dress him, they choose his home, his furnishings, his social activities, his iTunes playlist. Everything is arranged for him; he decides nothing himself. Clearly, such a person has abdicated the process of living. He has placed his life in the hands of others. He is technically alive, but he does not have a *human* life, any more than does someone in a permanent coma. No one's interests can be served by his willingly becoming a vegetable—even if just a part-time vegetable (as is usually the case with altruism's supplicants). To whatever extent a person accepts the premise that someone else is responsible for his life, he negates the value of living.

Every choice advocated by altruism is antithetical to the requirements of human life: parasitism rather than productiveness, dependence rather than independence, self-abnegation rather than self-esteem, equality rather than achievement, mercy rather than justice, need rather than desert, government control rather than political freedom. It is a preposterous contradiction for someone to say: "I endorse altruism because I will benefit from it." A code that execrates self-interest cannot be the vehicle for *achieving* anyone's self-interest.

In a free society the small number of innocent victims of misfortune who are truly unable to care for themselves will rely on private, voluntary assistance. They will seek help from family or friends and, if that is not forthcoming, from private charities. In a free society, private philanthropy has always been available. Only an embittered altruist—whose underlying attitude toward people is resentment for imposing upon him a duty to serve their needs—finds this hard to believe. Only an embittered altruist cannot conceive of orphans being kept from starving in the streets, not through government intervention, but through people's uncoerced generosity. (Even in America's mixed economy, where government throttles the generation of wealth and then taxes people heavily to support a vast welfare state, private charities receive hundreds of billions of dollars annually.[15])

But the dispensing of charity in a consistently capitalist society will be based on certain acknowledgements by the recipient: first, that he retains the responsibility to do all he can for himself; second, that his well-being rests on his benefactor's moral and political right to live selfishly; and third, that the aid he receives is the result of the donor's benevolence, not of some collectivist duty.

As to all the rest of the people, who do not require charity, what they need most is to be left free to live self-sustaining lives. They need the freedom to be as productive as their abilities allow. They need the freedom to supply and to work at remunerative jobs. They need the dynamism of a laissez-faire economy, in which everyone's standard of living continually rises. And in a fully free economy, where government regulation does not intrude, jobs are available for all who seek them—in the same way that the law of supply and demand ensures that there are enough eggs, shoes or cars, at a market price, for all who demand them. People do not need tuition grants, mortgage subsidies, crop supports, minimum-wage laws, corporate bailouts or government-supplied medical care. They need only to be allowed to keep the money they earn—the money that is now taken from them to pay for the vast array of "free" benefits.

The man who tries to survive by using force against others is supporting his own destruction by implicitly sanctioning the use of force against himself. The same is true of the man who tries to survive by receiving sacrifices. He is implicitly sanctioning a duty on his part to serve others. He is sanctioning *his* role as a sacrificial animal whenever people with needs come knocking at *his* door.

Under altruism you must sacrifice for the sake of whoever has a little less—of anything, i.e., money or skills or health or intelligence or ambition. Altruism amounts to the demand that you keep sacrificing until you reach the zero of total selflessness—a demand that can be satisfied only when there is nothing left to be given up. It is a code under which all must eventually be bled dry.

When the political realm is ruled by tyrants, who deny the individual the right to live his life and pursue his values, it is logical to conclude that the tyrants' goal is not the happiness of their citizens. When similar shackles exist in the moral realm, imposed under the tyranny of need, the same conclusion is warranted.

NINE

CHOOSING TO LIVE

AT THIS POINT YOU MAY BE ASKING YOURSELF WHY THE choice has to be so stark. Why must it be either/or, black or white? Doesn't life require navigation through shades of gray? Why shouldn't we travel a middle-of-the-road course, somewhere between complete selfishness and complete altruism?

Because in matters of *principle* any attempt to compromise is self-destructive.

If someone were to propose a law banning all books critical of the government, the proper response would not be to seek some middle ground, in which, say, criticism of foreign policy would be banned, but not of domestic policy. Such a response would concede the entire principle. It would grant government the right to censor our ideas, with some quibbling over the details. The imposition of total censorship would then become only a question of time.

Similarly, if police were to confront a burglar and "compromise" by allowing him to keep only half his loot, they would not be preserving 50 percent of the tenet of private property: they would be nullifying it completely. The truth—bromides to the contrary notwithstanding—does not invariably lie between two extremes. When it comes to principles, there is no "splitting the difference." As Ayn Rand put it: "There are two sides to every issue: one side is right and the other is wrong, but the middle is always evil."[1]

THE NEED FOR CONSISTENCY

There is no escaping this either/or. Either we have a right to our own existence or we don't. Either we are morally entitled to seek our own well-being or we must subordinate it to the demands of others. For every action we take and every goal we pursue, the standard we follow is either self-interest or self-sacrifice.

We can, of course, act inconsistently, sometimes following one standard and sometimes the other. That is what "gray" denotes—a mixture of what is clearly black and what is clearly white. In matters of ethics, to describe someone as gray is to say that his actions are morally self-contradictory.

While a code of self-sacrifice cannot be practiced consistently, a code of self-interest can, and must. Living requires rationality—and that means *unfailing* rationality. It requires a commitment to take all the actions necessary to sustain one's life. When crossing a busy street, you must *always* check for traffic; it takes only a single out-of-focus instant to get run over. It takes just a single dose of poison to be killed, no matter how many times in the past you have been careful about what you ingest. The pursuit of self-interest is a full-time job. Every lapse endangers that pursuit.

Consider this letter, published in an advice column, from a mother agonizing over which school to select for her children. She has enrolled them in a private school, but is troubled by the thought that she is acting selfishly. She feels a moral duty to support the public school system, even though she acknowledges that her children will receive an inferior education there. She describes her dilemma: "Will the kids attend public or private schools? Should one minimize the opportunities for one's own child in service to the greater good?"[2]

Because choosing a superior school conflicts with the demands of altruism, she is prepared to injure her own children. She is willing to sacrifice their cognitive development. Even if it means placing them in the company of incompetent teachers and apathetic students, she is ready to subordinate their welfare to some alleged greater good.

This woman seems to be a conscientious parent. She probably goes to great lengths to provide what is best for her children in regard to food, clothing, housing. But not in regard to education. There, she lets altruism rule. There, she counteracts her own values by acting *against* her children's best interests.

This is what gray people do regularly, when they jumble self-interest with self-sacrifice. They defeat their own good efforts. They undo their own accomplishments. To oscillate between egoism and altruism is to oscillate between advancing one's life and undermining it.

The question that should be asked is not why conflicting codes of behavior cannot be reconciled, but why anyone wouldn't *want* to practice selfishness consistently. Why would you value your life one day, yet be willing to surrender it the next? Why would you want to follow, even for a single step, a path consisting only of barriers to your happiness? Every element of the altruist philosophy clashes with the requirements of human living—a clash manifested not just in the explicit moral evaluations made by altruism, but in its implicit methodology, i.e., in its basic approach to reality. Let's look at an analogy in economics.

In his brilliant primer, *Economics in One Lesson*, Henry Hazlitt writes that the central error characterizing bad economics is myopia. People observe the breaking of a shopkeeper's window, for example, and conclude that the economy will be richer by virtue of the new business that will now accrue to a glazier. Or they look at the effects of war and claim that the work required to repair all the devastation will lead to an increase over pre-war production and employment. Or, in response to an increase in government spending, they applaud the newly created demand for goods and services.

These are all instances of the same mistake, Hazlitt says. The key to economics "consists in looking not merely at the immediate but at the longer effects of any act or policy; it consists in tracing the consequences of that policy not merely for one group, but for all groups."[3] That is, the money spent by the shopkeeper to repair his window is money that now cannot be spent on other goods. Had the breakage not occurred, he could have bought, say, a new computer. He, and the economy in total, would have had an intact window plus the computer. Now there is only the intact window. Similarly, the resources devoted to rebuilding a bombed factory are resources that, if not for the destruction, could have been used to expand the factory or to construct a second one. And with respect to the money spent by government, it is first taken from those who have earned it, and whose demand for goods and services correspondingly shrinks.

In other words, the purveyors of bad economics ignore what is not visible to immediate perception.

The same is true of the purveyors of bad ethics.

A proper ethics tells us to take a long-range, principled approach to life. It recognizes that human life requires production, and that production is the result of individual effort—the effort of every man who chooses to think and to act in order to generate the values that sustain life. When you put food on your table, a proper ethics recognizes that the food comes into existence because of the work of particular individuals, from farmers to truck operators, from seed developers to supermarket managers, from commodity traders to investment bankers—to you, who worked to earn the money that enables you to have ample food in your cupboard. A proper ethics recognizes that you exerted your effort, as did all the others in the chain of production, based on a dual premise: that everyone has the moral right to enjoy the fruits of his work, and that the political system will protect this right.

The altruist, however, is not concerned with any of the principles behind production. He sees only the brute fact that you now have plenty to eat while some homeless men down the block, or in some foreign nation, do not—and decrees that you must feed them. The altruist does not ask himself how the food got to your table. He is oblivious to cause-and-effect. He does not care to consider the cause of prosperity in capitalist, profit-driven countries or the cause of poverty in socialist, sacrifice-driven countries. The goods are here, he says—let's redistribute them. How did they get here? Somehow. How will we have the goods tomorrow, if producers are shackled to the needs of non-producers? "Tomorrow" is too much of an abstraction for the altruist.

The egoist ethics adopts the broad, conceptual approach appropriate to the existence of human beings. The altruist ethics takes the short-sighted, range-of-the-moment approach appropriate to the existence of animals.

The philosophic conflict between the two codes extends to a view of man's nature. Altruism describes man as belonging in one of two categories: an unthinking, helpless child, requiring a nanny-state to provide the goods and the guidance his life needs; or an unthinking, predatory beast, requiring the hovering presence of state regulators to restrain his animalistic impulses. The code of selfishness, however, regards man as an efficacious, independent, self-responsible being—as long as he chooses to exercise his rational faculty.

Similarly, the two codes reflect two opposing views of the nature of the world. Altruism sees the universe as an inhospitable place, where misery and despair are man's normal condition. We are impotent, according to altruism, doomed to tormented, anxiety-driven lives—as aptly conveyed in Edvard Munch's famous painting, *The Scream*. We must endure a lifeboat existence, tossed by the waves of a malevolent universe, incapable of planning our futures, perpetually dependent upon others to rescue us from looming calamity. We must view other people not as partners in production and trade, but as unwanted bodies that are taking up our boat's limited space—bodies that, should we choose to be "selfish," must be thrown overboard.

The philosophy of egoism, by contrast, sees the world as harmonious with man's aspirations—as a place where values are attainable and happiness is achievable, where man can live in accord with the demands of nature, where the interests of rational individuals do not conflict, where interactions between people result in gains for all, where disappointment and pain arise but are surmountable by thinking human beings, where life does not consist of endless emergencies and where man's central purpose is not to avert disaster but to seek joy.

The ethics of self-interest is an ethics of idealism. It regards man as noble—as both able and worthy to live, provided he chooses to live by reason. If he acts by the judgment of his mind and by the standard of his life, man can live successfully and ethically. He does not have to take a cynical view of principles, as something to be publicly espoused and privately scorned. He can fully embrace morality because the moral, in this code, is the practical.

Authentic egoism is characterized not by a crude materialism, but by the integration of material and spiritual values, fueled by the knowledge that one's material values are the product and the expression of the virtues created in one's own character. The selfish individual regards material goods, not as something to be gotten by any means, but as something to be *earned*, by means of honest, productive action.

Egoism is morally demanding, and morally rewarding. It requires you to regard yourself not as congenitally incompetent or congenitally corrupt, but as someone who can make himself both capable and worthy of living. Egoism enables you to experience self-esteem, because it views the self as morally good. It allows you to take pride in what you've made of your life. It tells you to live, not as a mendicant—not by sacrificially "casting your bread upon the waters" and then waiting in turn to receive the sacrifices made by others—but as a self-reliant, self-confident individual who seeks what he deserves, no less and no more.

MAKING THE CHOICE

If you take ideas seriously, you want to set a principled course for your life, rather than to drift aimlessly, moved by your mood of the moment. You realize the importance of choosing—of consciously, deliberately choosing—the moral system you will follow.

And if you want an existence of meaning and purpose, and know you can't find it in the ruinous platitudes of altruistic service—if you are willing to think for yourself, rather than uncritically accept the beliefs of others—you will challenge the dogmas of tradition. You will ask yourself why a code of sacrifice and suffering and submission is preferable to one that says your life and your mind are your own, too precious to be surrendered.

If you do decide to adopt a morality under which your own life is your highest value, don't be deterred by the smears you will inevitably encounter. You will advocate a philosophy that respects the sovereignty of each individual—but you will be called a hater of humanity. You will advocate a philosophy that supports man's inalienable right to his liberty and to his property—but you will be called a proponent of enslavement and thievery. You will advocate a philosophy of laissez-faire, prohibiting all government interference in private, peaceful activities—but you will be called an autocratic fascist. You will advocate a philosophy that demands an unwavering commitment to moral principles such as honesty and integrity—but you will be called an amoral reprobate. You will advocate a philosophy of reason—but you will be called a wanton, do-whatever-you-feel-like emotionalist.

Your only defense against such accusations is to point dispassionately to the facts—and to deal with people to whom facts matter.

Your intellectual adversaries will try to cloud the facts with their disingenuously ambiguous terminology. Don't let them get away with it. Be unequivocally clear on the meaning of the concepts you use.

Don't describe your dedication to personally beneficial values as a sacrifice. Your willingness to forgo immediate gratification, in anticipation of greater long-term rewards, is an act of *selfishness*. When you trade something you value less for something you value more—when, for instance, you give up your nights and weekends in order to acquire the skills for a new career—you are profiting, not sacrificing. Similarly, when you feed and clothe your children, you are not sacrificing. You've chosen to value them because they are *your* children. If you were to keep them hungry and naked so that you could feed and clothe needy children elsewhere—*that* would be a sacrifice.

Don't describe the irrational as selfish. A crook is not pursuing his long-range interests. Neither is a drug addict or a compulsive gambler or a continually mooching relative. They are all evading the requirements of human living and are acting in contradiction to their genuine self-interest.

Don't describe love or friendship as self-sacrificial. It is the opposite: a discriminating relationship you choose to enter into with someone who is of particular, personal value *to you*.

Don't describe benevolence as equivalent to altruism. Altruism does not mean giving a starving man some food, but having a *duty* to do so, disdainful of your own well-being. It means that his need creates a moral claim against you. Choosing to help someone who is in distress through no fault of his own, if you can afford to do so, is an act of goodwill, based on a bond of shared (actual or potential) values. Altruism, however, insists that you *surrender* your values—that it is more desirable to give to a stranger than to a friend, to an enemy than to a stranger, to the guilty than to the innocent, to the undeserving than to the deserving. Altruism is the demand that you be indentured to the misery of others. But a servant who provides for his master's needs is *not* engaging in an act of benevolence.

Above all, don't try to appease the apostles of altruism. Don't try to justify your actions by declaring that they benefit society. Every rational value you produce does indeed benefit others, but such benefit is not the *standard* by which your actions should be judged. Your life is an end in itself, and its justification does not lie in any service you provide to others. The composer of a symphony enhances the lives of many people, from music publishers to the ushers who will find employment in a concert hall that performs his work. But they are not the purpose, or the moral validation, of his efforts. He does not tailor his music to their needs; he does not, for example, tack on an extra movement so that ushers can work additional hours. The composer acts for his own gain, and so do you—and you should not hesitate to say so.

Don't apologize for being selfish. Be proud of it. Be proud of the fact that you refuse to surrender the inestimable value that is your life and the inviolate purpose that is your happiness. Be proud of the fact that you have chosen to live—not as a self-effacing, life-renouncing serf, but as a self-respecting, life-affirming human being.

NOTES

CHAPTER 1

1. Abbott v. Bragdon, 163 F.3d. 87 (1st Cir. 1998), http://law.justia.com/cases /federal/appellate-courts/F3/163/87/494494/ (accessed November 2, 2012). The ruling said that once public officials declare that the chances of infection are insignificant, the dentist's own judgment about the degree of risk he faces is to be ignored.
2. Ian Austin, "B.C. League Bans Boys' Team for Big Wins," *National Post* (Canada), December 8, 2004, p. A1.
3. Mohandas Gandhi, quoted in Charles W. Byrd, *If Only That Horse Were a Member of My Church* (Lima, Ohio: CSS Publishing Co., 1988), p. 92.
4. Ruth Shalit, "Defining Disability Down: Why Johnny Can't Read, Write, or Sit Still," originally published in *The New Republic*, August 25, 1997, republished on the Hoover Institution's website, http://media.hoover.org /sites/default/files/documents/0817928723_239.pdf, p. 243 (accessed October 15, 2012).
5. Ibid., p. 244.
6. Rami Rabby, letter to the editor, *New York Times*, June 7, 1989, http://www .nytimes.com/1989/06/07/opinion/l-airlines-discriminate-against-the-bli nd-029489.html?scp=2&sq=senate%20committee%20backs%20bill%20 on%20blinds%20rights%20in%20airliners&st=nyt (accessed November 2, 2012).
7. "Senate Committee Backs Bill on Blind's Rights in Airliners," *New York Times*, May 17, 1989, http://www.nytimes.com/1989/05/17/us/senate-committee -backs-bill-on-blind-s-rights-in-airliners.html?scp=7&sq=senate%20com mittee%20backs%20bill%20on%20blinds%20rights%20in%20airliners &st=nyt (accessed November 2, 2012).
8. Associated Press, "Couple Meet, Forgive Slayer of Daughter, 20" *Los Angeles Times*, January 16, 1978, p. B3.
9. Carl Hulse, "Battle on Estate Tax: How Two Well-Organized Lobbies Sprang into Action," *New York Times,* June 14, 2002, p. A34.

CHAPTER 2

1. Friedrich Nietzsche, *The Anti-Christ*, trans. R. J. Hollingdale (London: Penguin Classics, 1990), p. 127.
2. Thomas Hobbes, *Leviathan* (Indianapolis: Hackett Publishing, 1994), pp. 75–76.
3. Ayn Rand, *The Virtue of Selfishness* (New York: Signet, 1964), pp. 13–35. See also Leonard Peikoff, *Objectivism: The Philosophy of Ayn Rand* (New York: Meridian, 1994), Chapters 7 and 8.
4. Rand, *The Virtue of Selfishness*, p. 21.
5. Ayn Rand, *The Fountainhead* (New York: Signet, 1952), pp. 195, 196, 197.
6. Mark Curnutte, "Selfishness Gets the Blame," *Cincinnati Enquirer*, January 2, 2007, http://www.enquirer.com/editions/pdf/OH_CE_020107.pdf (accessed January 5, 2007).
7. Auguste Comte, *A General View of Positivism*, trans. John Henry Bridges (New York: Cambridge University Press, 2009), p. 18.
8. Ibid., p. 13.
9. Auguste Comte, *Passages from the Letters of Auguste Comte*, trans. John Kells Ingram (London: A. & C. Black, 1901), p. 56.

CHAPTER 3

1. Ayn Rand, *For the New Intellectual* (New York: Signet, 1961), pp. 126–127.
2. "Fire Marshal Charged with Setting Stony Brook Fire," *Stony Brook Statesman*, January 19, 1983, p. 12, http://dspace.sunyconnect.suny.edu/bitstream/1951/28429/1/Statesman%2c%20V.%2026%2c%20n.%2042.pdf (accessed March 21, 2013). See also David Goldman, "Malpractice: Press Looks Into S.B.'s Hiring Practices," *Stony Brook Press*, January 27, 1983, p. 3, http://dspace.sunyconnect.suny.edu/bitstream/1951/37555/1/Stony%20Brook%20Press%20V.%2004,%20N.%2013.PDF (accessed March 21, 2013).
3. Associated Press, "Minnesota Man Charged in Killing of Second Honeywell Co-Worker," *New York Times*, July 25, 1988, http://www.nytimes.com/1988/07/25/us/minnesota-man-charged-in-killing-of-second-honeywell-co-worker.html (accessed April 12, 2011).
4. Ian Parker, "The Gift," *The New Yorker*, August 2, 2004, pp. 57–58.
5. Stephanie Strom, "An Organ Donor's Generosity Raises the Question of How Much Is Too Much," *New York Times*, August 17, 2003, http://www.nytimes.com/2003/08/17/us/an-organ-donor-s-generosity-raises-the-question-of-how-much-is-too-much.html (accessed March 21, 2013).
6. Ibid.
7. Parker, "The Gift," p. 62.
8. Jerry Schwartz, "Generous to a Fault, or Faulty Generosity?," *Los Angeles Times*, November 30, 2003, http://articles.latimes.com/2003/nov/30/news/adna-giver30 (accessed March 24, 2013).
9. General Assembly of Pennsylvania, House Resolution No. 422, September 30, 2003.

10. Strom, "An Organ Donor's Generosity."

11. Steven Greenhouse, "Overweight, but Ready to Fight," *New York Times*, August 4, 2003, pp. B1, B5.

12. Walter Olson, "Disability Law Protects Bad Doctors," *New York Times*, November 28, 1997, http://www.nytimes.com/1997/11/28/opinion/disabilities -law-protects-bad-doctors.html (accessed March 24, 2013).

13. Associated Press dispatch quoted in Daniel Seligman, "Only in America," *Fortune*, November 5, 1990, p. 187.

14. See Ayn Rand's "The 'Conflicts' of Men's Interests," in *The Virtue of Selfishness* (New York: Signet, 1964), pp. 50–56.

15. Peter Singer, "What Should a Billionaire Give—and What Should You?," *New York Times Magazine*, December 17, 2006, p. 63.

CHAPTER 4

1. Fund-raising letter (undated) from Connecticut Public Television, with the heading: "PLEASE NOTE: This is not a bill! But we hope you'll send a check just the same." It is signed by the current (2014) CEO, Jerry Franklin. (Letter received in the mail by the author, date unknown.)

2. Sheryl Gay Stolberg, "Ease a Little Guilt, Provide Some Jobs: It's Pork on the Hill," *New York Times*, December 20, 2003, pp. A1, A13.

3. Ibid.

4. Office of United States Senator Robert Byrd, "Byrd on Funding for Mother's Day Shrine," news release, accessed via WSAZ News Channel 3 (Charleston, West Virginia), March 14, 2008, http://www.wsaz.com/political/news releasesheadlines/16679301.html (accessed April 3, 2008).

5. "FY 2007 Grant Awards: Literature Fellowships for Translation Projects," National Endowment for the Arts, http://www.nea.gov/grants/rece nt/07grants/LitTranslation.html (accessed March 13, 2008).

6. B. Drummond Ayres, Jr., "Political Briefing; Lose Those Tattoos, with Federal Help," *New York Times*, January 20, 2002, http://www.nytimes .com/2002/01/20/us/political-briefing-lose-those-tattoos-with-federal-he lp.html (accessed March 25, 2013).

7. Ibid.

8. Responsible Wealth, "Forbes 400 Richest Americans: They Didn't Do It Alone," news release, September 24, 2004, http://faireconomy.org/press_ro om/2004/forbes_400_richest_americans_they_didnt_do_it_alone (accessed March 26, 2013).

9. Gary Olson, "Wealthiest Americans Owe Nation a Dividend," *The Morning Call* (Lehigh Valley, Pennsylvania), May 17, 2007, http://www.mcall.com /news/opinion/anotherview/all-left_col-a.5852503may17,0,4343922.story (accessed May 19, 2007).

10. Herbert Simon, "UBI and the Flat Tax," *Boston Review*, October/November 2000, http://bostonreview.net/BR25.5/simon.html (accessed March 27, 2013).

11. "Anti-copyright," *Wikipedia*, http://en.wikipedia.org/wiki/Anti-copyright# Authorship_and_creativity (accessed July 14, 2014).

12. "The Coming of Copyright Perpetuity," editorial, *New York Times*, January 16, 2003, p. A28.

13. From an *amicus* brief, not filed, by Mark Rothe, Esq., on behalf of the Family Research Council in the case of *Washington v. Glucksberg*, http://wings .buffalo.edu/faculty/research/bioethics/brf-roth.html (accessed March 27, 2013). The brief was written for the U.S. Supreme Court's October 1996 term (though the Family Research Council ultimately decided not to include this brief in its filing). The Supreme Court, reversing the Ninth Circuit Appeals Court, ruled that there is no constitutional right to commit suicide, 521 U.S. 702 (1997).

14. Ibid. The original source is Edward Hyde East, *Pleas of the Crown*, vol. I (London: J. Butterworth and J. Cooke, 1803), p. 219.

15. Georg Wilhelm Friedrich Hegel, *Philosophy of Right*, trans. T. M. Knox (New York: Oxford University Press, 2007), p. 241.

16. Ibid., p. 156.

17. W. T. Stace, *The Philosophy of Hegel: A Systematic Exposition* (New York: Dover Publications, 1955), p. 425.

18. "Social Security Ballots," editorial, *Washington Post*, October 29, 1982, p. A28.

19. Georg Wilhelm Friedrich Hegel, *The Philosophy of History*, trans. J. Sibree (New York: Cosimo, 2007), p. 46.

20. Hegel, *Philosophy of Right*, p. 196.

21. Stace, *The Philosophy of Hegel*, p. 406. (The quote is from Stace, attributing the idea to Hegel.)

22. Newton Minnow, "Television and the Public Interest," speech to the National Association of Broadcasters, Washington, D.C., May 9, 1961 (the famous "vast wasteland" speech), http://www.americanrhetoric.com/speeches/new tonminow.htm (accessed March 27, 2013).

23. William E. Kennard, "Fox and NBC Renege on a Debt," op-ed, *New York Times*, October 3, 2000, http://www.nytimes.com/2000/10/03/opinion/fox -and-nbc-renege-on-a-debt.html (accessed March 28, 2013).

24. Gary Thatcher, "In the Soviet Union, Every Candidate for the Parliament Is a Front-runner," *Christian Science Monitor*, March 1, 1984, http://www .csmonitor.com/1984/0301/030117.html (accessed March 28, 2013).

25. John Dewey, "My Pedagogic Creed," *The Early Works of John Dewey*, vol. 5, ed. Jo Ann Boydston (Carbondale, Illinois: Southern Illinois University Press, 2008), p. 86.

26. Ibid., p. 89.

27. Ibid., p. 84.

28. John Dewey, *The School and Society*, ed. Jo Ann Boydston (Carbondale, Illinois: Southern Illinois University Press, 1980), p. 11.

29. Ibid., p. 20.

30. Neal Boortz, "Socialism Being Taught in Elementary Schools," *NewsMax*, September 18, 2000, http://archive.newsmax.com/articles/?a=2000/9/18/1 34737 (accessed March 28, 2013).

31. Dewey, *The School and Society*, pp. 10–11.

32. Ayn Rand, "America's Persecuted Minority: Big Business," *Capitalism: The Unknown Ideal* (New York: Signet, 1967), p. 61.

CHAPTER 5

1. John Locke, *The Second Treatise of Government*, ed. Thomas P. Peardon (Indianapolis: Bobbs-Merrill, 1952), p. 17.
2. Auguste Comte, *The Catechism of Positive Religion*, trans. Richard Congreve (London: John Chapman, 1858), pp. 332, 333.
3. Saint Augustine, quoted by Pope John Paul VI in *Populorum Progressio (On the Development of Peoples)*, a papal encyclical, Item No. 23, issued March 26, 1967, http://www.vatican.va/holy_father/paul_vi/encyclicals/documents/hf _pvi_enc_26031967_populorum_en.html (accessed April 2, 2013).
4. Proverbs 3:5.
5. Thomas Jefferson to his nephew, August 1787, in *The Portable Thomas Jefferson*, ed. Merrill D. Peterson (New York: Penguin Books, 1977), p. 425.
6. Ayn Rand, "Man's Rights," in *The Virtue of Selfishness* (New York: Signet, 1964), p. 93.
7. The Rockefeller Foundation, *The Use of Land: A Citizen's Policy Guide to Urban Growth*, 1973, quoted in "Property—Is Private Ownership Outdated," *The Reporter* (a newsletter published by the Pacific Legal Foundation), July/August 1980, p. 1.
8. Stephen Holmes and Cass R. Sunstein, *The Cost of Rights: Why Liberty Depends on Taxes* (New York: W. W. Norton & Co., 1999), pp. 17, 219.
9. Rand, "Man's Rights," pp. 92, 93.
10. For a fuller discussion of the basics of capitalism—including analyses of the common evils falsely attributed to capitalism—read Ayn Rand's *Capitalism: The Unknown Ideal*, Henry Hazlitt's *Economics in One Lesson*, Ludwig von Mises' *Planning for Freedom* and Frederic Bastiat's *Economic Sophisms*.
11. Rent Stabilization Association of New York, "We're All for Rent Control," full page ad, *New York Times*, May 5, 1986, p. B10.
12. Michael Barbaro, "Wal-Mart Counters Criticism with a Political-Style Ad Campaign," *New York Times*, August 29, 2006, p. C3.
13. Angus Maddison, *The World Economy: A Millennial Perspective* (Paris: OECD Publishing, 2001), p. 263; Angus Maddison, *The World Economy: Historical Statistics* (Paris: OECD Publishing, 2003), p. 613.
14. Maddison, *The World Economy: A Millennial Perspective*, p. 32.
15. United States Census Bureau, "World Population: Historical Estimates of World Population," http://www.census.gov/population/international/data /worldpop/table_history.php (accessed May 8, 2013). This is based on a population of 40 million in 1200 B.C. and 900 million in 1800 A.D., compared with 1.75 billion in 1910.
16. Ayn Rand, *Atlas Shrugged* (New York: Signet, 1964), pp. 451–452.

CHAPTER 6

1. Cass R. Sunstein, *The Second Bill of Rights: FDR's Unfinished Revolution and Why We Need It More Than Ever* (New York: Basic Books, 2006), p. 13.
2. John Shattuck (former director of the Washington office of the American

Civil Liberties Union), interview by Robert Pear, "The Main Civil Liberty: A Right Not to Starve," *New York Times,* July 18, 1984, p. A14.

3. "A Catholic Framework for Economic Life," statement issued by the National Conference of Catholic Bishops, November 1996, http://www.usccb.org/issues-and-action/human-life-and-dignity/economic-justice-economy/catholic-teaching-on-economic-life.cfm (accessed March 31, 2002).

4. "33-Stone Man Sues Over Detention," BBC News, February 22, 2005, http://news.bbc.co.uk/2/hi/uk_news/england/southern_counties/4287377.stm (accessed August 27, 2011).

5. Jens F. Laurson and George A. Pieler, "The Government That Stole Christmas," *Forbes,* December 23, 2009, http://www.forbes.com/2009/12/23/christmas-charity-scrooge-government-opinions-contributors-laurson-pieler.html (accessed March 30, 2013).

6. "What of the Children Left Behind?" editorial, *New York Times,* June 17, 1991, p. A14.

7. Jonathan J. Cooper, "States Target Payday Lenders and Their High Rates," *Seattle Times,* April 8, 2010, http://seattletimes.nwsource.com/html/businesstechnology/2011561955_paydayloans09.html (accessed March 30, 2013).

8. David Leonhardt, "Budgets Behaving Badly," *New York Times,* December 3, 2008, pp. B1, B7.

9. Richard H. Thaler and Cass R. Sunstein, *Nudge: Improving Decisions About Wealth, Health and Happiness* (New Haven: Yale University Press, 2008), pp. 19–20. (It is worth noting that Sunstein served as the Obama administration's "regulation czar" from 2009 to 2012.)

10. Ibid., p. 22.

11. Denise Grady, "FDA Pulls a Drug, and Patients Despair," *New York Times,* January 30, 2001, http://nytimes.com/2001/01/30/health/30drug.html?pagewanted=3 (accessed March 30, 2013).

12. Ibid.

13. Ibid. (One-and-a-half years later the FDA allowed the drug to be sold—but only under highly restrictive conditions.)

14. Fran Hawthorne, *Inside the FDA: The Business and Politics Behind the Drugs We Take and the Food We Eat* (Hoboken: Wiley and Sons, 2005), p. 28.

15. Here are just four egregious examples of FDA-mandated delays:

- After clinical testing showed that Provenge, a novel vaccine for advanced prostate cancer, increased patients' survival rate, the FDA's own advisory panel in March 2007 voted 13 to 4 to endorse the drug's effectiveness, and 17 to 0 to endorse its safety. Nonetheless, the FDA refused to approve the drug until April 2010. During those three years, close to 100,000 people in the United States died of prostate cancer. Obviously, no one can know precisely how many might have been helped by the drug; all one can know for sure is that none were allowed to find out. See "Prostate Cancer and FDA Politics," editorial, *Wall Street Journal,* April 20, 2009, http://online.wsj.com/article/SB124018504363133253.html (accessed March 31, 2013).

- Kadcyla, a drug to treat advanced breast cancer, was approved in February 2013. The manufacturer had asked for accelerated approval in August 2010, after initial testing showed that it reduced tumors in one-third of patients whose condition had worsened following prior treatment with an *average of seven drugs* (including the three most commonly used chemotherapy agents). But the FDA refused, claiming that "all available treatment choices . . . had not been exhausted in the study population." Ohad Hammer, "Immunogen: What Really Happened with T-DM1's Filing?," Seeking Alpha, September 1, 2010, http://seekingalpha.com/article/223275-immunogen-what-really-happened-with-t-dm1s-filing (accessed March 31, 2013); "FDA Denies Accelerated Approval of Genetech's Trastuzumab-DM1 (T-DM1) BLA for Metastic Breast Cancer," *News Medical,* August 27, 2010, http://www.news-medical.net/news/20100827/FDA-denies-accelerated-approval-of-Genetechs-trastuzumab-DM1-(T-DM1)-BLA-for-metastatic-breast-cancer.aspx (accessed March 31, 2013). Again, it is impossible to calculate exactly the harm and the early deaths suffered by cancer patients during this delay. But approximately one million women have breast cancer at any given time, of whom 15–20 percent have the specific type of cancer Kadcyla is designed to treat and were denied its benefits for two-and-a-half years. See "State Cancer Profiles: Prevalence Projections Report by State 5-Year Prevalence Counts: Female, Breast Cancer, All Ages Sorted by Projected Counts 2014," National Cancer Institute, http://statecancerprofiles.cancer.gov/prevalence/index.php?duration=5&statistics=0&age=001&type=prev&stateFIPS=00&cancer=055&sex=2&sortVariableName=default&sortOrder=default (accessed March 26, 2013); "Treatment of Metastatic HER2-Positive Breast Cancer," Cancer.Net (accessed March 26, 2013). http://www.cancer.net/research-and-advocacy/asco-care-and-treatment-recommendations-patients/treatment-metastatic-her2-positive-breast-cancer (accessed February 14, 2015).
- Beta blockers, a variety of drugs designed to treat heart attacks, were available in Europe in 1967, but were not approved by the FDA until 1976. Just one of those drugs, according to the medical researcher who originated the concept of a U.S. "drug lag," could have saved 10,000 lives a year. See Sam Kazman, "Deadly Overcaution: FDA's Drug Approval Process," *Journal of Regulations and Social Costs,* September 1990, pp. 42–43, also at http://cei.org/pdf/3887.pdf (accessed March 31, 2013).
- Spina bifida is the most common disabling birth defect in the United States, affecting approximately 3,000 pregnancies (both full-term and aborted) annually. Folic acid (a B-vitamin) was found in the early 1980s to reduce the risk of spina bifida. But the FDA *prohibited companies from publicizing this information*—even though the federal government's own Centers for Disease Control and Prevention was recommending, by 1992, that women of childbearing age take folic acid supplements to prevent birth defects. Then, displaying the utter arbitrariness of its powers, the FDA reversed itself in 1996, first allowing and later *requiring*

manufacturers to fortify various grain products with folic acid. During the subsequent ten years, spina bifida cases *dropped by over 30 percent* (from 26.36 per 100,000 births in 1996 to 17.99 in 2006). See "Spina Bifida," American Pregnancy Association, http://www.american pregnancy.org/birthdefects/spinabifida.html (accessed October 10, 2012); T. J. Matthews, "Trends in Spina Bifida and Anencephalus in the United States, 1991–2006," Centers for Disease Control and Prevention, http://www.cdc.gov/nchs/data/hestat/spine_anen/spine_anen.htm (accessed October 10, 2012).

(Of course, the proper solution to this deadly problem is not to "streamline" the FDA's bureaucratic procedures, but to *eliminate* them and allow private parties to judge the suitability of medications.)

16. "Organ Donation and Transplantation Statistics," National Kidney Foundation, http://www.kidney.org/news/newsroom/factsheets/Organ-Donation -and-Transplantation-Stats.cfm (accessed June 25, 2014).

17. Social Security Administration, "The 2012 Annual Report of the Board of Trustees of the Federal Old-Age and Survivors Insurance and Federal Disability Insurance Trust Funds" (as of January 2012), p. 65, http://www.ssa .gov/oact/TR/2012/tr2012.pdf (accessed January 16, 2013).

18. Savings are the source of investment, which the creation of a nest egg requires. When someone privately saves for retirement, the capital ordinarily remains intact, generating returns by being continuously put to productive use. Social Security collects over $800 billion annually in payroll taxes (including Medicare). See "2014 Federal Budget in Pictures," The Heritage Foundation, http://www.heritage.org/federalbudget/federal-revenue-sources (accessed March 31, 2013). This money, instead of being injected productively each and every year into the economy and raising everyone's standard of living, is *not* invested, but is immediately consumed. So over $15 billion of what should be permanent wealth is dissipated weekly. Madoff's schemes, by comparison, resulted in the dissipation of about $20 billion of wealth *in total*. See Aaron Smith, "Billions of Dollars Slated for Madoff Victims," *CNN Money*, July 26, 2012, http://money.cnn.com/2012/07/26/news/companies/madoff -victims/index.htm (accessed March 31, 2013).

19. An average worker who began in 1967 and retired in 2011 at age 66 after 44 full years of employment will have paid $138,948 into the Social Security fund (including the employer's share), based on a constant tax rate of 12.4 percent and on the median income in U.S. Census Bureau's "Table H-10, Age of Head of Household by Median and Mean Income," http://www.census.gov/hhes /www/income/data/historical/household/ (accessed November 26, 2012). He will receive monthly benefits of $1,853. See "Social Security Quick Calculator," Social Security Administration, http://www.socialsecurity.gov /OACT/quickcalc/ (accessed November 26, 2012). Had this worker instead been allowed to invest his payments in the S&P 500 or in corporate AAA bonds, he would—based on average returns from 1967 to 2011—have had a capital fund upon retirement of $998,900 (S&P 500) or $660,000

(bonds), a fund non-existent under Social Security. See "Compound Annual Growth Rates (Annualized Return)," *Moneychimp*, http://www.money chimp.com/features/market_cagr.htm; "Selected Interest Rates (Daily)—H.15: Historical Data," Federal Reserve, http://www.federalreserve.gov /releases/h15/data.htm; "Moody's Seasoned Aaa Corporate Bond Yield," Federal Reserve Bank of St. Louis, http://research.stlouisfed.org/fred2 /series/AAA/downloaddata?cid=119; "Moody's Seasoned Aaa Corporate Bond Yield," *Ycharts*, http://ycharts.com/indicators/moodys_seasoned_aaa _corporate_bond_yield (accessed February 20, 2015). From this fund, he could decide to buy an immediate annuity, which would pay him a lifetime monthly benefit of $4,700 on the S&P investment (*two-and-a-half times more* than Social Security) or $3,100 on the bond investment (*two-thirds more* than Social Security), http://www.ImmediateAnnuities.com (accessed January 3, 2013). (The annuity calculations are based on a New York State Joint Life Income Annuity, as of January 2013, where 100 percent of the lifetime income is paid to the survivor; if both beneficiaries die before receiving an amount equal to the premium paid, other designated beneficiaries would receive payments equaling the balance of the premium.)

20. Ayn Rand, *For the New Intellectual* (New York: Signet, 1961), p. 25.
21. Andrew Pollack, "FDA Restricts Access to Cancer Drug, Citing Ineffectiveness," *New York Times*, June 18, 2005, http://query.nytimes.com/gst/fu llpage.html?res=9A0DE4DD153BF93BA25755C0A9639C8B63 (accessed April 1, 2013).
22. Andrew Pollack, "Panel Advises FDA to Narrow Its Approval for Avastin," *New York Times*, June 29, 2011, p. B3.
23. Ibid.
24. Ibid.
25. Duff Wilson, "On Sexual Desire Drug for Women, FDA Panel Says More Study Is Needed," *New York Times*, June 19, 2010, p. B3.
26. Duff Wilson, "Maker's Push for a Pill Stirs Debate on Sexual Desire," *New York Times*, June 17, 2010, p. A3.
27. Scott Travis, "District Weighs Community Service Requirement," *South Florida Sun Sentinel*, December 16, 2002, http://articles.sun-sentinel.com /2002-12-16/news/0212160127_1_school-board-school-employees-gradua tion (accessed April 1, 2013).
28. Warren Buffett, "My Philanthropic Pledge," *CNNMoney*, June 16, 2010, http://money.cnn.com/2010/06/15/news/newsmakers/Warren_Buff ett_Pledge_Letter.fortune/index.htm?postversion=2010061608 (accessed November 27, 2010).
29. *The Speeches of Adolf Hitler*, ed. N. H. Baynes, vol. I, 1922–39 (Oxford: Oxford University Press, 1942), pp. 871–872.
30. *Lenin's Collected Works*, ed. Jim Riordan, vol. 28 (Moscow: Progress Publishers, 1965), pp. 62–75.
31. *Selected Works of Mao Tse-tung*, vol. 3 (New York: Pergamon Press, 1967), p. 267.

32. Duncan Christy, "General Walters at the U.N.," *M* magazine (published by Fairchild Publications; ceased publication in 1992), March 1986, p. 82.

33. Rudolf Hoess, *Commandant of Auschwitz: The Autobiography of Rudolf Hoess* (London: Weidenfeld and Nicolson, 1959), p. 197.

34. Gary L. McDowell, introduction to *Reason and Republicanism: Thomas Jefferson's Legacy of Liberty,* ed. Gary L. McDowell and Sharon L. Noble (Lanham, Maryland: Rowman and Littlefield, 1997), p. 2.

35. Michael F. Holt, *Franklin Pierce* (New York: Times Books, 2010) pp. 53–54.

36. Thomas Jefferson, quoted in Elizabeth Campbell, introduction to *The Jefferson Bible: What Thomas Jefferson Selected as the Life and Morals of Jesus of Nazareth* (Thousand Oaks, California: Lakewood Publishing, 2011), p. 1.

CHAPTER 7

1. Richard Ralston, "The Orange Grove: FDA as Drug Research Censor," *Orange County Register,* March 4, 2009, http://www.ocregister.com/opinion/drug-25762-patients-drugs.html# (accessed June 23, 2014). While nominally allowing medical literature to be distributed to doctors, the FDA, in a 2009 policy statement, imposes severe restrictions on such literature—from prohibiting discussion of any clinical investigation that the FDA has previously decided "is not adequate and well-controlled," to requiring that the disseminated material be accompanied by other literature (if available) "that reaches contrary or different conclusions," to forbidding the contents from being "highlighted, summarized or characterized by the manufacturer." (Minor modifications to its 2009 policy were being considered by the FDA in 2014.) See "Guidance for Industry," Food and Drug Administration, http://www.fda.gov/regulatoryinformation/guidances/ucm125126.htm (accessed June 25, 2014).

2. Doug Beazley, "Prison Guards Forbidden to Wear Protective Gear," *Calgary Sun,* March 17, 2004, p. 16.

3. Diane Ravitch, *The Language Police: How Pressure Groups Restrict What Students Learn* (New York: Vintage Books, 2004), p. 10.

4. "Teaching Emotive and Controversial History," a report commissioned by Britain's Department for Education (London: The Historical Association, 2007), p. 15, http://www.history.org.uk/file_download.php?ts=1204732013&id=784 (accessed June 13, 2014).

5. Pope Innocent III, *Two Views of Man,* trans. Bernard Murchand (New York: F. Ungar Publishing Co., 1966), pp. 5, 9.

6. William F. (Billy) Graham, "Learn the Lesson of the Worm," in *A Treasury of Great American Speeches,* ed. Charles Hurd (New York: Hawthorn, 1970), p. 340.

7. Matthew 5:43–44.

8. Aristotle, *The Nicomachean Ethics,* ed. Lesley Brown, trans. David Ross (Oxford: Oxford University Press, 2009), p. 69.

9. Ayn Rand, *The Virtue of Selfishness* (New York: Signet, 1964), p. 27.

10. Ayn Rand, *For the New Intellectual* (New York: Signet, 1961), p. 131.

11. Ayn Rand, *The Fountainhead* (New York: Signet, 1952), p. 376.

12. "Jonestown," *Wikipedia*, http://en.wikipedia.org/wiki/Jonestown (accessed May 24, 2013); "Alternative Considerations of Jonestown and Peoples Temple," San Diego State University, http://jonestown.sdsu.edu/?page_id=35332 (accessed June 15, 2014).

13. Andrea Sachs, "Q&A: A Jonestown Survivor Remembers," *Time*, November 18, 2008.

14. Roger Cohen, "Why? New Eichmann Notes Try to Explain," *New York Times*, August 13, 1999, pp. A1, A3.

15. Gail Buckley, "Charity Begins at Home, and You Live in the World," *New York Times*, December 3, 2003, p. E8.

16. Rudolf Hoess, *Commandant of Auschwitz: The Autobiography of Rudolf Hoess* (London: Weidenfeld and Nicolson, 1959), p. 160.

17. Eugene Davidson, *The Trial of the Germans* (Columbia, Missouri: University of Missouri Press, 1997), pp. 237–238.

CHAPTER 8

1. Union County High School (Liberty, Indiana), "Community Service" form for students, http://www.uc.k12.in.us/clientuploads/UCHS/CommunitySe rvice[1].pdf (accessed March 21, 2013).

2. Barbara Hagenbaugh, "Nation's Wealth Disparity Widens," *USA Today*, January 22, 2003, http://www.usatoday.com/money/economy/fed/2003-01 -22-household-study_x.htm (accessed March 21, 2013).

3. Steven Greenhouse, "Corporate Greed, Meet the Maximum Wage," *New York Times*, June 16, 1996, http://www.nytimes.com/1996/06/16/weekin review/corporate-greed-meet-the-maximum-wage.html?module=Search& mabReward=relbias%3Ar (accessed June 16, 2014).

4. Steve Stecklow, "Finnish Drivers Don't Mind Sliding Scale, but Instant Calculation Gets Low Marks," *Wall Street Journal*, January 2, 2001, http://online.wsj.com/article/SB978398058976592586.html (available to non-subscribers via: http://www.stayfreemagazine.org/public/wsj_finland.html) (accessed March 21, 2013).

5. Immanuel Kant, *Foundations of the Metaphysics of Morals*, trans. Lewis White Beck (New York: Bobbs-Merrill, 1959), p. 14.

6. William A. Henry III, *In Defense of Elitism* (New York: Doubleday, 1994), p. 133. The book recounts how in November 1992 Shannon Merryman, a deaf-mute high school student in Bristol, Rhode Island, gained the right to enter a national *oratory* contest, sponsored by the Veterans of Foreign Wars. The contest required submissions via audiotape. Originally, her proposal to make a presentation not orally but in American Sign Language, on videotape, was turned down. After being sued in federal court for discrimination, the sponsor gave in, allowing her "speech" to be delivered on audiotape by an interpreter.

7. John Taylor, "Are You Politically Correct?," *New York* magazine, January 21, 1991, p. 34, quoted in Smith College Office of Student Affairs, "Specific Manifestations of Oppression," circular.

8. "School Boards Will Recognize Other Cultures, but as Inferior," *New York Times*, May 13, 1994, http://www.nytimes.com/1994/05/13/us/school-boa

rd-will-recognize-other-cultures-but-as-inferior.html (accessed October 26, 2012).

9. Amy Harmon, "How About Not Curing Us, Some Autistics Are Pleading," *New York Times,* December 20, 2004, http://www.nytimes.com/2004/12/20 /health/20autism.html?_r=1&scp=1&sq=alternative%20form%20of%20 brain%20wiring&st=cse (accessed March 21, 2013).

10. "Autism Rights Movement," *Wikipedia,* http://en.wikipedia.org/wiki/Auti sm_rights_movement (accessed March 21, 2013).

11. Felicity Barringer, "Pride in a Soundless World: Deaf Oppose a Hearing Aid," *New York Times,* May 16, 1993, pp. 1, 22.

12. Edward Dolnick, "Deafness as Culture," *The Atlantic Monthly,* September 1993, p. 37.

13. Barringer, "Pride in a Soundless World."

14. Dolnick, "Deafness as Culture."

15. Eduardo Porter, "The Role, and Limits, of Charity," *New York Times,* November 14, 2012, pp. B1, B8.

CHAPTER 9

1. Ayn Rand, *For the New Intellectual* (New York: Signet, 1961), p. 173.

2. Patty Stonesifer and Sandy Stonesifer, "A Private Matter," My Goodness, *Slate,* April 1, 2009, http://www.slate.com/articles/life/my_goodness/2009 /04/a_private_matter.html (accessed June 26, 2014).

3. Henry Hazlitt, *Economics in One Lesson* (New York: Three Rivers Press, 1988), p. 17.

INDEX

Age of Reason, 102
Agriculture, Department of, 129
Altruism:
  as antipode of production, 121
  as antithetical to requirements of
    life, 65, 204–205
  and assault on self-esteem, 180–183
  as based on faith, 36–38, 100
  and cannibalism, 54, 93
  as causing perpetual conflict, 64–65
  as code of *dis*values, 196
  as duty to serve others, 6–10
  and "economic rights," 128–129
  as emotionalism, 37, 57–59
  and envy, 189–190, 194
  and equality of income, 116–117,
    191–193
  as false basis of capitalism, 119–120
  vs. generosity, 8
  and "giving back," 166–168
  "good" defined as harmful under,
    196
  and incompatibility with freedom,
    95–98
  as injurious even to recipient of
    sacrifice, 202–205
  misconceived as respect for rights, 6
  and moral-practical dichotomy, 47
  as moral sanction for dictators,
    171–172
  and nature of man and reality,
    214–215
  no guidance for living offered by, 65
  no validation for, 36
  pain as measure of virtue under, 196
  and parasitism, 202
  and perverse meaning of "need,"
    10–13
  as primacy of need, 15, 90
  and range-of-moment approach,
    214
  redistribution of wealth under, 193
  as rejecting self-responsibility, 203
  as requiring sacrifice of one's moral
    principles, 50
  and sacrifice of the mind, 177–180,
    185–188
  universal acceptance of, 5, 16–18
  and view of man as helpless,
    130–132
America, 127, 128, 168
  as founded on individualism, 174
  as founded on philosophy of rights,
    102–103, 112–113
  ideals of contradicted by altruism,
    175–176
  as partly free and partly controlled,
    114
  as republic, not democracy, 112
  as welfare (or "entitlement") state,
    127–128
American Civil Liberties Union, 128
Ancient Greece, 101
Aristotle, 40
  as advocate of rational egoism,
    24–25